A PORTRAIT OF
MOLOKAI
Collector's Edition

A peaceful and tranquil setting of the graveyard at Kalawao, Kalaupapa, with Molokai's North Shore in the background.

JAMES H. BROCKER

Halawa Bay,
East Molokai.

DEDICATION

This book is dedicated to Maria Thompson. Without her constant encouragement and enduring confidence in me, this publication would still be sitting on the back burner of my old camp stove. It is also dedicated to my mother, Ruth Francis, and to the memory of my father, Herman Theodore, for their guidance and training during my early years, which have allowed me to accomplish the goals in life that I have achieved so far.

ABOUT THE AUTHOR

Born and raised of German ancestry in the farm and ranching country of central Texas, the author received his formal education at Sam Houston University, majoring in Business Administration and History. He is a Federal Aviation Administration certified Airline Transport Pilot in single and multi-engine aircraft, a Commercial helicopter pilot, and also is a Certified Flight and Ground Instructor in single and multi-engine jet and propeller driven fixed wing aircraft and helicopters.

During his diversified flying career, he has logged over 13,000 hours of flight time world-wide, including pilot training for South American governments and extensive flying throughout the South Pacific. He served as an airport manager for several years as well.

The author also holds an Advanced Open Water Dive License with the Professional Association of Dive Instructors.

The author has called Hawaii his home since the 1960's. He moved from Honolulu to the Island of Molokai in the late 1970's, and after a time, put aside his flying career to establish several corporations in the retail and wholesale trade. Among his hobbies are raising rare and exotic tropical parrots, photography, horticulture and fishing.

ACKNOWLEDGMENTS

A special thanks to Ellen Osborne, whose skilled and tireless efforts transcribed these writings into computer form for publication.

PHOTOGRAPHY

All photographs in this book were shot with a Canon A E-1 camera using 24 through 300 mm lens and were taken by James H. Brocker unless otherwise noted.

Inside front cover photo:
Kapuaiwa "Coconut Grove"
Inside back cover photo:
Moaula Falls, Halawa Valley

Distributed by
Molokai Fish & Dive Corporation
P. O. Box 576
Kaunakakai, Hawaii 96748
(808)-553-5926
and by
Booklines Hawaii, Ltd.
94-527 Puahi Street
Waipahu, HI 96797-4208
(808) 676-0116

Copyright 1994 by James H. Brocker
UPC #79437300000
I. S. B. N. # 0-9642197-0-0
Publisher: Molokai Fish & Dive Corporation
First Printing, 1995.

TABLE OF CONTENTS

▼▼▼▼▼▼▼▼▼▼▼▼▼▼▼▼▼▼

PREFACE

▼▼▼▼▼▼▼▼▼

Commonly called the "Friendly Island" by the rest of the state, Molokai's population, which is yet to exceed 10,000, is comprised of almost half native Hawaiians. It is probably the most Hawaiian of all the islands, with the exception of the privately-owned Island of Niihau. 37 miles long, never more than 10 miles wide at any one point, it is the fifth largest island in land area of the Hawaiian chain.

Only 26 miles from the busy metropolis of Honolulu, this quiet little island lies sleepily lost and forgotten among the bright lights and highly publicized commercial ventures and attractions of its bigger sisters, Kauai, Oahu, Maui and the Big Island of Hawaii.

After a 20-minute flight from Oahu, stepping off the plane onto Molokai is like turning back time 50 years when the world was indeed a friendlier and less hurried place. The island is unspoiled, low key, and an atmosphere of tranquility and purposefulness seems to hang heavy in the salt air. Molokai is truly a world apart from the Hawaii that is the weekly scene on TV shows or found passing hurriedly through Waikiki.

It is a place where smiles come easily and effortlessly, and a hand wave from a moving car is more common than a blinking turn signal or an angry honking horn.

In the days of the ancient Hawaiians, Molokai was held in great respect and fear, not only for the peoples' expert skills in the art of warfare, but also as a stronghold of powerful kahunas (healers and sorcerers) and mighty heiaus (temples) that were used in the worship of various Hawaiian gods. Still, after hundreds of years, these stone heiaus can be seen throughout the island, bearing mute testimony to the religions and customs of long ago. Over the decades there were many fierce battles fought along the shores and surrounding ocean, to repel armies from neighboring islands that sought to extend their rule over the rich lands and productive waters of Molokai.

Prior to the arrival of the white man, agriculture played a large role in the economy and survival of the island. During those times, wealth was measured by the amount of food that an area could produce and, with this system, Molokai indeed was a very wealthy island. Crops consisted of sweet potato, banana, sugar cane, and many varieties of taro. Its aquaculture during that time was highly perfected, and even now the remains of many of the fishponds can be observed along the southeastern shore.

Molokai today is an agricultural center with thousands of pounds of watermelon, bell peppers, onions, green beans, coffee and herbs grown and exported to outside islands and the mainland by both large and small-scale farmers. The likelihood of Molokai becoming the bread basket of Hawaii seems to be ensured.

There are also several large world-wide corn companies that are taking advantage of the fertile soil and ideal growing conditions to cultivate experimental high-yield hybrid corn. These seeds are sold to corn producers in the global market. In fact, a large portion of the 80 million acres of corn production in the United States saw the beginning part of its development on Molokai.

The main center of activity and shopping on Molokai is the town of Kaunakakai. Its two short blocks have virtually remained unchanged since the 1920's and somewhat resemble a set from an old Western movie. Those of the action crowd will be somewhat disappointed, as much of the island rolls up the carpet at 6:00 every evening, and on a Sunday afternoon in town, you would almost expect to see a tumbleweed rolling lazily down a deserted street. The only exception to Sunday afternoon traffic is an occasional lonely dog in search of leftovers on a plate lunch. Even on the busiest of days you will never find a traffic jam on the two lane roads, nor will you find a single traffic light on the entire island.

Now let's begin our journey...

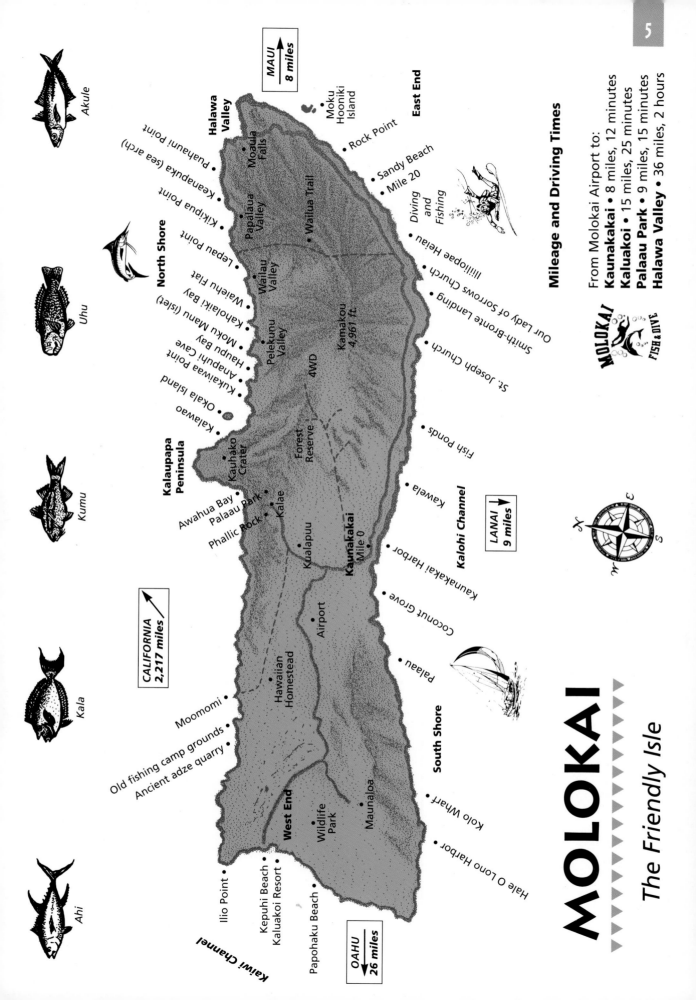

MOLOKAI
The Friendly Isle

Akule

Uhu

Kumu

Kala

Ahi

MAUI
8 miles

Halawa Valley

Moku Hooniki Island

East End

Moaula Falls

Rock Point

Sandy Beach
Mile 20

Diving and Fishing

Puahaui Point

Keanapuka (sea arch)

Kikipua Point

Papalaua Valley

Wailua Trail

Iliiliopae Heiau

North Shore

Lepau Point

Waiehu Flat

Kahoiaiki Bay

Wailau Valley

Smith-Bronte Landing

Our Lady of Sorrows Church

Moku Manu (islet)

Haupu Bay

Anapuhi Cave

Pelekunu Valley

Kamakou 4,961 ft.

St. Joseph Church

Kukaiwaa Point

4WD

Okala Island

Kalawao

Kauhako Crater

Kalaupapa Peninsula

Forest Reserve

Fish ponds

Awahua Bay

Palaau Park

Kalae

Kawela

Phallic Rock

Kualapuu

Kaunakakai Mile 0

Kaunakai Harbor

Kalohi Channel

LANAI
9 miles

Coconut Grove

Moomomi

Hawaiian Homestead

Airport

Palaau

CALIFORNIA 2,217 miles

Old fishing camp grounds

Ancient adze quarry

South Shore

West End

Wildlife Park

Maunaloa

Kolo Wharf

Ilio Point

Kepuhi Beach

Kaluakoi Resort

Papohaku Beach

Hale O Lono Harbor

Kaiwi Channel

OAHU 26 miles

Mileage and Driving Times

From Molokai Airport to:
Kaunakakai • 8 miles, 12 minutes
Kaluakoi • 15 miles, 25 minutes
Palaau Park • 9 miles, 15 minutes
Halawa Valley • 36 miles, 2 hours

MOLOKAI
FISH & DIVE

CHAPTER 1 · WEST END

▼▼▼▼▼▼▼▼▼▼▼▼▼▼▼▼▼▼▼

Desolate rolling hills laced with intricate violet wildflowers and bursts of tall range grass flow like waves of water across the lands known today as the West End of Molokai. When a rare shower falls upon this open range of low lying mountains and prairies, parched vein-like gorges trickle with fresh water and empty all too soon into the powerful sea, leaving the land as suddenly as it came.

Roughly 1,800,000 years ago, a large fiery volcano spewed forth its glowing molten lava and created half of the diverse face of Molokai. This entire side of the island beholds an innocent and undisturbed presence. Perhaps it is because the ancient hula is said to have originated on the hills of Maunaloa, overlooking the deep life-giving waters below. Or maybe it is because Papohaku, the most magnificent beach in Hawaii, lies undisturbed here, fronting three miles of stunning coastline. Strangely, though, it remains undiscovered, for it is rare to find even the remains of lonely footprints etched in the ivory sands or to find a visitor enjoying the immaculate campground.

Secret heavenly coves offer remote sanctuaries for solitude among protruding lava rock points and cobblestoned ocean bottoms. Northeast tradewinds roar through the low shrub hunting grounds and hit the faces of incoming ocean swells, creating offshore conditions ideal for surfers and boogie boarders. The small and alluring Kepuhi Beach harbors the Kaluakoi Resort, the only refuge for visitors fortunate enough to have discovered the magic of Molokai's West End.

Fifty-three thousand acres of lush pastureland belong to the Molokai Ranch, where large herds of domesticated cattle roam along with the secretive spotted axis deer. An exotic wildlife park within the ranch is home to giraffes, Barbary sheep and many other wild animals from their native lands of Africa and Asia.

And then there is Moomomi, an area rich in Hawaiian history and ancient rituals. This stretch of coastline was used for gathering food and hosts many human burial sites within its ever-shifting sand dunes.

Adjacent to this area are the bounteous and fruitful agricultural farms of the Hawaiian Homesteaders, dedicated to perpetuating the ancestral belief that being connected with the earth is essential and is a trait inherent in being a Hawaiian.

Yes, the West End holds infinite gifts and mesmerizes all who take but a moment to contemplate its pure and rugged beauty.

◄

Outrigger canoes lay idle, awaiting the day their bows will be turned westward toward the Island of Oahu.

▲ Molokai's major link to the outside world is the Hoolehua Airport, which divides the island's West End from its central area. Flights are offered only during daylight hours for passengers as well as freight, including the daily newspaper. On most weekends you will find "standing room only" at the small terminal as "off island" people escape the big city for rural Molokai.

▶

▶ Leaving the airport, a home-made sign on vacant land seems to have a dualistic meaning with respect to both traveling on Molokai's two-lane highway and the unhurried lifestyle that is offered on the island.

◄ Vast open chaparral areas of the West End are ideally suited to host the abundant groups of wild Axis deer which roam freely. Originally from India, a small herd of these animals was given to King Kamehameha V in the 1860's. Since then, under ideal conditions, the population has multiplied dramatically.

▲ As the 5 o'clock rush hour approaches, this is the traffic you can expect to encounter leaving the airport and heading toward the West End of the island.

◄ Western Molokai mountain ranges offer a panoramic view of Hawaiian Homestead lands and central and upper Molokai. In the distance twenty miles away is the Forest Preserve and Kamakou, the highest elevation on the island, at 4,961 feet.

▶

This world-class 18-hole golf course is located at the Kaluakoi Resort complex on the western shore of Molokai. The resort area features several condominiums and one hotel. Shopping is somewhat limited for the visitor, but the trade off for seclusion is definitely worth it.

▶

Located at Kaluakoi, this brilliantly colored bougainvillea, rugged lava rock, and ivory white sand provide an exotic collaboration of color, complimenting the turquoise surf.

▶

Pohuehue, the beach morning glory, is a perennial seashore vine that extends over the ground as far as 100 feet. It thrives in the hot, sandy areas of Hawaii's beaches and can be found island-wide on Molokai.

◄ Winter's pounding surf is made for watching, not swimming, and should be approached with caution because of its strong undertow. In the foreground a small lava rock sea arch weathers the pounding sea with Puu O Kaiaka towering above in the distance.

◄ The true wealth of Molokai's gold is brought forth in the glory of its unequaled radiant sunsets. Each one is a different and unique experience to behold.

▲ Kepuhi Beach at Kaluakoi is a pleasant spot to take a quiet walk, read a book, or perhaps work on your suntan. Be careful along all of the West End shores - the surf and strong current can be treacherous.

▲ Obviously by this boy's grin he, like his friend, has no thought of Monday morning or the studying that goes along with it. Gliding down the face of emerald green waves is all that's on his agenda.

▶ A boogie board, a pair of duck feet, and the water are all that are necessary for this Molokai lad to enjoy a Saturday after having his head filled with school-work and books for an entire week.

▲ Frozen for a moment in time, this talented surfer has just finished an exhilarating ride on one of Molokai's winter waves. The winter surf in Hawaii is much more powerful and challenging than the calmer swells that occur during the summer months.

▲ While the boys are surfing, three local girls seem to be having a lot of fun making small splashes in big waves! A day at the beach for Molokai people is always filled with playful happiness for all.

◄

Playing it safe, this visitor seems quite content to watch the activity from the waters' edge.

Those of the older set seem more content with trying to catch something for dinner. This woman uses a 20-foot fiberglass fishing rod so she can get her hook and line into the water beyond the lava rock outcroppings.

▼

▶ Papohaku Beach Park is the only public campground on Molokai's West End. For overnight camping a permit from the state is required. During the day, however, the park can be used without a permit. There are restroom facilities, barbecue pits for cooking, and shade trees to provide relief from the hot sun.

▶

Dramatic contrasts, such as this West End coast, reflect Molokai's diverse and ever-changing scenery. Here, the lack of abundant rains have quickly turned this small riverbed into crackly, parched clay.

▼

◀ Enjoying a quiet stroll along the water's edge, this native California girl decided to move to Molokai and reside at the young age of 19, because as she puts it, "Surfing and diving in an unspoiled paradise is what life's all about for me."

▲ Papohaku Beach, 3 miles long and 300 feet wide, is one of the longest natural beaches in the Hawaiian Island chain. Unspoiled and lacking any footprints, on a really crowded day you might encounter a total of 2 or 3 people having all of this breathtaking beauty to themselves.

▲ Although normally an unsafe anchorage for transient boats because of rough seas and high winds, the waters off western Molokai can bestow calm conditions for brief periods of time, offering the crew of a passing vessel a picture-perfect memory to last a lifetime.

▲ Molokai Ranch offers guided tours of their 400-acre wildlife park. More than a thousand African and Asian animals roam freely within an area of terrain and vegetation that closely resemble their native habitat. Pictured here are three Barbary sheep, the only sheep native to Africa.

▶

One of the several gentle giraffes at the park that visitors can feed from a bowl (if they care to), and which always seem more than willing to show their best side for photographers.

▲ The oryx, with its sharp pointed horns, are native to Africa. There, they are highly prized by the native tribes who use the horns for spear tips and tools.

◄

Along the western shore, this little cove is so typical of the many quiet and secluded beaches to visit, where a person can get away from it all.

◄

On Molokai, as well as in all of Hawaii, most children learn to trust the water before they learn to walk. This Molokai family is enjoying the water together at a weekend outing near Dixie Maru beach.

◄

The ever-changing moods of Molokai's sunsets are just as diverse and grand as the seemingly endless variations of its land-scapes and terrain.

▶ Cattle ranching is done throughout Molokai, from very small operations to Molokai Ranch's enormous 53,000 acre parcel, partially pictured here along the sloping crest of the west Molokai mountains.

▲ From the Maunaloa area on most days, looking beyond the prime grazing land toward the west, you can see the Island of Oahu. Its famous landmark, Diamond Head, 30 miles away, is visible on the left, and at night the entire island glitters with the sparkling of big city lights.

▶ These giant Norfolk pines tower over the older residential houses that make up the little hilltop town of Maunaloa.

▲ Once a thriving pineapple plantation town in the 1920's, Maunaloa drowsily overlooks most of the West End ranch land and the Kaluakoi resort area. It is said that in this district the birth of the hula originated and spread throughout the other Hawaiian Islands.

▲ No automatic garage doors for this fire station. Seldom used, this one tanker truck station serves the needs of western Molokai. When necessary, other trucks from Kaunakakai and Kualapuu can be brought in to help fight any fires that may occur.

▲ Like old soldiers standing in their final formation, these broken and battered surfboards are silent reminders of big waves and better days, when they were both new and strong.

▶

Framed within their fence of surfboards, these two friendly local maidens are enough to brighten up any landscape with their warm and open smiles.

There are months of long, hard training, usually after normal working hours, to prepare teams for the annual Molokai to Oahu outrigger canoe race. This event is a true test of sheer physical stamina and human will that tests the limits of endurance to the very edge.

The race begins at Hale O Lono Harbor on Molokai's southwest shore at dawn, with a crowd of onlookers and team members. The supercharged excitement and mood that fills the early morning air on that day can only be described as intense! The longest time for crossing the channel was 8 hours 55 minutes, in 1952. The shortest record-breaking time of 4 hours 55 minutes occurred in 1993.

Held during Aloha Week every year since 1952, the 41-mile Molokai to Oahu canoe race has brought as many as 75 teams from all over the world. The competition entails paddling their outrigger canoes over the treacherous Kaiwi Channel with waves so high at times that sight of these long canoes will be lost as they top one wave and descend to the bottom of the next one.

▲ An aerial view of a few agricultural plots, located in Hawaiian Homestead land near the airport. Under the 1921 Hawaiian Homes Act, 40-acre homestead plots are given to those people qualifying with enough percentage of Hawaiian blood to build their homes and cultivate the land.

▶

Serving the rural needs of the Hawaiian Homesteaders is the Hoolehua Post Office. To increase business at their small country office, they offer "Post A Nut," where they will give you a free Molokai coconut and for a few dollars postage, mail it with your personal message and Aloha to anywhere in the U.S.A.

▶

This fella was found guarding the entrance to his master's agricultural fields. He seems to be wishing someone would turn on the air conditioner and bring him some ice cold water to quench his thirst.

◀ Dryland and wetland taro prosper throughout the Island of Molokai. Shown here is the dryland variety with some of its edible leaves harvested. Taller plants are normally planted on both sides as a windbreak protection from the strong winds that frequently blow here.

▲ Sometimes called the "Bread Basket of Hawaii," Molokai is a leading exporter in the state for thousands of pounds of succulent watermelon. Often at the peak of the growing season, a tub of a hundred or so melons will be left by one of the growers along the side of a well-traveled road, for everyone's free and pleasurable use.

▲ The papaya tree, which produces a melon-like sweet fruit, is very easily grown. Commonly seen along road sides, papaya seeds merely thrown on the ground will most often produce a fruit-bearing tree such as this, within a few short months.

▶ This Tongan family grows yams for export. In Tonga, this giant variety is reserved only for the king and high dignitaries at special occasions. The yam will grow to a length of five feet and weigh as much as 100 pounds. It takes a strong man about an hour to dig one of these huge edible roots from the ground.

▲ Two Tongan women of Molokai hold up tapioca, a staple food of the South Pacific. The delectable root is either boiled or steamed and eaten throughout the South Seas very much like rice is consumed in the Hawaiian Islands.

▶ Did you ever think that pigs would eat coconuts? They obviously have no complaints with this supplement to their diet of grains and vegetables. Within a few short months these porkers will attain the weight of three hundred pounds and make their appearance as "guests of honor" at a Molokai luau.

▲ Master fisherman, hunter, and Hawaiian Homestead farmer, Kelii (on the right) and a friend stand in his front yard among many of his gill fishing nets made of white monofilament and lobster nets of orange nylon.

▲ Drying in the sun, each of these gill nets is 100 feet long and many feet deep. When dispersed into the ocean at dusk, these nets are filled with fish by the time they are brought up at dawn. The fish not used in home consumption by family or friends are sold to the stores, restaurants and hotels on Molokai.

Bountiful farms and agricultural plots regress into pastureland nearing the coastal cliffs of Homestead Lands. Relentless northeast tradewinds whirl salt in from the Pacific Ocean, making most of the land near the palis (cliffs) unfit for cultivation.

▲ No longer serving a purpose, an old fencepost marks some unused and forgotten boundary approaching the steep cliffs located near Moomomi Bay.

Just as the map makers of old told how one would fall off the face of the earth after reaching a certain point, so seems to be the fate of any explorer who reaches the northern edge of Molokai Homestead land.

These graceful horses are free to roam over acres of wide open range land. In the distant background is the west Molokai mountain range, leading down to the Kaluakoi resort and the quaint town of Maunaloa.

Undisturbed, this is a place of solitude and quietness where only the winds whisper of their distant travels. Beyond and barely visible on the horizon is the Kalaupapa peninsula.

The Moomomi Bay area is held sacred by Hawaiians in honor of their ancestors who once came to the region to gather salt and food from the sea. It is a habitat rich in the bones of long-extinct and only recently discovered birds, and there are many human burial sites scattered throughout the rolling windswept sand dunes.

The Moomomi area also was used for the quarrying of stone to make adzes which were vital to the early Hawaiians as a tool for producing items needed in their everyday life. This area was never densely populated, but was used as a place that the people from other districts visited periodically because of its rich fishing grounds.

From Ilio Point on Molokai's northwestern tip to the red-hued flames of the setting sun, nothing stands between, except countless miles upon miles of vast open ocean.

CHAPTER 2 · CENTRAL & UPPER MOLOKAI

The area known to some as middle and upper Molokai begins where the rolling hills and agricultural lands of western Molokai merge with the foothills of the mountains of eastern Molokai. The powerful and steady trade winds that blow across the northern cliffs and down the sloping sides of the precipitous eastern mountains bring with them frequent rains that shower the area for a number of miles westward.

By the time the exhausted winds reach the edge of the Hawaiian Homestead lands, however, they have lost most of their moisture, and water must be piped in to suffice the needs of the resident farmers. Along with the persistent breeze comes the crisp and sometimes chilly air that this region is well known for. One can literally taste the difference in the air as they begin the climb toward the mountains, departing the hot, drier climate below.

Central and upper Molokai are composed of three distinct and different sectors: the cool, damp Kualapuu - Kalae - Palaau area, the dry, scrub brush Red Hill area, and the thick, wet Forest Preserve region.

The first district is a deep sea of ever-changing hues of green, and the only one of the three which has had much settlement to speak of over the years. Its upper hills, deep in legends and ancient history, were once the home and dwelling place of the alii (chiefs and ruling class), as well as the location for an advanced school of hula and the honored games of peace.

The area of Kalae today is mostly settled by non-Hawaiians, some of whose families have lived there for over a century. Other newcomers have only recently established themselves. As with all the other communities on Molokai, each population within an area holds a very high regard to their land and believe it to be the best locale in all of Molokai.

The Red Hill vicinity is arid and uninteresting, except to those hunters who venture into the thorny thickets in search of game. The rugged, auburn soil is dehydrated and hosts a maze of kiawe trees and smaller shrubs. Throughout history, Red Hill and its surrounding proximity have never been settled much; the area was used mostly as a transient area for people passing through from one district to another.

The Forest Preserve gradually ascends to tower above both Kualapuu - Kalae - Palaau and the Red Hill districts. It is the largest, most pristine, and least settled land on all of Molokai. Very little information was written or passed on regarding the early usage of the upper reaches of this vast forest and bog habitat.

Signs of early Hawaiian life are few, most likely due to the heavy amounts of rain and moisture which made the rain forest fit only for the occasional harvesting of wild foods.

In the early 1900's, large tracks of land in its lower portion was reforested to create more of a water shed in hopes of reversing the deforestation of the previous century. All of Molokai receives a portion of its water, in one manner or the other, from the rains that are produced within these mountains, including the dry but expanding resort developments on the shores of the West End.

Today much of the upper reaches are under the control of the Nature Conservancy, which has the responsibility of ensuring its preservation in a natural state.

▶ Numerous acres of open fields between the airport and Kaunakakai lay empty except for tufts of range grass. In the far distance on the right, the Island of Maui is barely visible under a layer of clouds. Looking to the left, the island's topography gradually ascends toward the Molokai Forest Preserve.

▲ Used in the days when autos were fewer and slower, an old bridge with its embankment walls made of hand-laid stone is now only a reminder of the road that once carried traffic westward out of Kaunakakai.

▶ Somewhat aged and faded, but still full of life and ready to go at a moment's notice, this fire truck stationed near the town of Kualapuu deals with the occasional needs of Hawaiian Homestead Lands and central and upper Molokai.

Within the small plantation town of Kualapuu is the Kualapuu Cookhouse, widely known and enjoyed by locals and visitors alike. The town itself, with a population of around 500, has a small post office, one grocery store with limited staples, and a single octane gas pump.

Found in great numbers, the mynah bird was imported to Hawaii from India in 1865 to combat army worms that were killing the lawns. Like the egret, they have created more problems than they have solved because of their spreading of unwanted vegetation through their droppings.

A rope, a tire, and a fine old tree; how many countless hours of happiness and enjoyment this spot must render for some boy or girl, aspiring their young dreams and making their youthful plans.

▶ Constructed near the town of Kualapuu, this 1,400,000 gallon reservoir is the largest rubber-lined water tank in the world. It is fed by waters from the rain forest high above in the mountains and deep underground pools that are tapped by wells. Water from here is then distributed to the vast agricultural plots located to the west.

▲ Replacing Molokai's pineapple industry in the Kualapuu area, coffee production has begun to take root as the number one crop. Row after row of lush coffee plants stretch over the rolling highland hills. Plants reach a maximum height of 12 feet and begin to produce beans when they are about two feet tall.

▶ Since the beans of the coffee tree, called cherries, ripen at different times, they must be picked by hand in order to gather only the ripe fruit. Pruning must be done after the yearly harvest as the mature branches only bear fruit once.

An old fence along a single lane road in upper Molokai brings images to mind of dusty and tired cowboys of the old west, tying up their horses to the rail and ambling through a pair of swinging doors to wet their parched throats.

Sparsely populated, the upcountry of Kalae was formerly the dwelling place of ancient Hawaiian chiefs. A Hawaiian game called Ulu Maika was also played in this general vicinity. Beyond the Norfolk pine trees in the distance are the steep cliffs that descend to the Kalaupapa Peninsula.

As if balancing the Island of Lanai on its top, this small volcanic dome of 1,210 feet, officially named Puu Luahine, is commonly referred to as Red Hill by the local population. It lies within a state game management area and is visible from all surrounding areas.

▲ Well-known for its locally frequent rains and cool temperatures, Kalae has abundant grazing pastures for cattle and horses. There are also large numbers of wild deer and pig that range freely throughout the sparsely fenced and open woodlands.

▶ New life springs to an old kiawe wood fence post as it plays host to lichen and other forms of plant life that seemingly exist without any soil, drawing the breath of life only from the heavy amounts of precipitation in the air.

▲ Christmas Berry shrubs can be found along the roadsides of much of Molokai. They bloom during the fall and produce an inedible but beautifully colored red berry that is quite often used in decorations during the island's Christmas season.

▲ Rudolph Meyer, an immigrant from Germany, constructed the Meyer Sugar Mill in 1878. It was operated until 1889 and utilized an animal-powered cane crusher and a steam engine for processing sugar cane. Listed on the Register of Historical Places, the Meyer Sugar Mill is now a public museum.

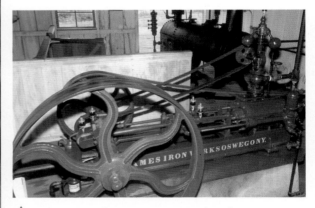

▲Built in 1879 by Ames Iron Works of Oswego, New York, the still working steam engine and boiler of the sugar mill has a single cylinder, six horsepower engine that runs at 175 rpm and produces 125 lbs. per square inch of pressure.

◀

Cattle egrets were originally imported to Hawaii to help control flies that damage the health and hides of cattle. These quick learners can be found on the backs of cows and horses, as well as browsing through freshly mowed grass, feeding on insects. This particular egret has unusual salmon-colored markings, atypical of the ordinarily all-white bird.

▶

Ti plants in Hawaii are respected as a source of good luck. They are frequently used in the blessing of a new home, boat, business, or anything else deemed important. They are used for wrapping food for cooking, and in the past, even as plates from which to eat. Ti leaves can be red or green, the latter being the most common and can be found growing in most yards on Molokai.

▲ Evergreen trees are perfectly adapted to the cool temperatures and ample rainfall of the higher elevations. These 70-foot Norfolk Island pines in Kalae on the way to the Kalaupapa Lookout are an impeccable example.

▲ The antlered memories of past deer hunts and many fine meals hang sunbleached from this small windmill in the backyard of a local resident.

▲ Throughout Molokai, citrus trees bear immense fruit, none quite so large as in the cool areas of Kalae. These lemons, the size of softballs from the author's yard, are being gathered by his kokua (helper). As with most things in abundance on Molokai, what is not needed is shared with friends and strangers alike.

The lights of Oahu, fifty miles away, are easily seen on clear nights from certain locations in Kalae. Especially beautiful are the holidays, when large amounts of fireworks are exploded into the air. In the distance, Moomomi Bay is visible as well as the rolling hills of Molokai's West End.

Upper Molokai, even today, has a haunting reputation of mystical legends and happenings. It is said by some that the presence of the Night Marchers of Molokai, the spirits of ancient Hawaiian warriors, can be felt as they make their silent way along the old trails on their journey to Moomomi. At times, a heavy fog-like mist rolls in over the area so thick that it is impossible to see beyond a few feet.

Moody and sullen days here can transform as suddenly as the blink of an eye to one that seems as if the heavens have opened up and lit a giant fire to warm the chill of the night. This picture and the previous two were shot on different days from the same location at the author's home. Note how Diamond Head on Oahu is clearly visible on the horizon.

▲ Guava fruit trees grow wild throughout Molokai and can be found readily along the Kalae highway. Guava was introduced to the Hawaiian Islands sometime before 1800 and is the most common wild fruit in Hawaii. The delicious pulpy and seedy fruit can be eaten raw or processed into juices and jams.

▲ When the guava fruit drops from the tree to the ground, wandering groups of wild pigs move into this area to feed greedily, until all the ripe fruit is gone. Sometimes it is possible to see one of these short, stocky creatures darting hastily into the brush along the roadside.

▲ Located near the end of Kalae highway at Palaau Park, the picnic pavilion area is a beautiful 34-acre retreat surrounded by thick growths of aromatic eucalyptus, ironwood, cypress and paper bark trees. It is best to dress warmly during a visit here, as the weather is somewhat cooler than the lower elevations.

▲ Keep a watchful eye around this road sign near the beginning of the Kalaupapa Trail, as sure-footed mules are used to carry day workers, supplies, and visitors from "Topside" Molokai to the Kalaupapa settlement some 1,600 feet below.

▲ Commuting to and from work at Kalaupapa on a daily basis, this man and his transportation are entirely a world apart from those having to contend with the freeways, traffic snarls and pollution associated with "fast lane" living.

▲ The trail, three miles long with twenty-six different switchbacks, has been in daily use for many decades to carry needed supplies as well as news to the isolated population there. Besides riding mules, the trail can be walked; however, permission is needed before entering the settlement from the Kalaupapa Department of Health or from a tour operator located within the settlement.

▲ An old, gentle dog spends his sleepy retirement waiting faithfully at the top of the trail each day for his master's return trip, as well as the love and affection that comes along with it.

The road to the Kalaupapa Lookout abruptly ends here among the paper bark and cypress trees. The best time to visit the Lookout is normally during the morning hours, when clouds are less prevalent than they are in the afternoons, and when rainfall is less likely to occur.

▲ A full moon in Palaau Park with the winds flowing through the paper bark trees has a way of making one's senses perk up to the extreme - even more when it is combined with the thick layers of fog common here, as it hangs suspended from the trees to ground level.

Located 200 yards from the Kalaupapa Lookout is the Phallic Rock. In ancient times it was looked upon as a symbol of generative power where offerings were made by the Hawaiians to achieve fertility. Phallic stones are fairly common in the islands; this one, however, is Hawaii's finest example. ▼

▲ Kalaupapa Lookout offers a spectacular view of the 4 1/2 mile peninsula where sufferers of Hansen's Disease, or leprosy, were exiled for life beginning in the 1860's. Today, most patients now are free to come and go as they wish. The settlement and its surrounding area are under separate control from the rest of Molokai by the State of Hawaii and maintained by the National Park Service.

◄

On Molokai, as well as throughout all of Hawaii, weddings are often performed outdoors among the endless green landscape and the gentle tradewinds that flow across it. Beginning their new life together, this happy bride and groom chose to say their vows under the Ironwood trees overlooking Kalaupapa at Palaau State Park.

▶

Remote and inaccessible sea cliffs that tower above the Kalaupapa Peninsula were one of the original considerations for the establishment of a leper colony there. The only way in at that time, other than a boat on a raging ocean, was by the narrow trail chiseled into the steep face of the cliffs by ancient Hawaiians, hundreds of years before.

▶

It is now possible to take a plane down to the settlement for a tour, rather than walking or riding a mule down the steep trail. Descending toward the Kalaupapa Airport on a quick seven-minute flight from Hoolehua Airport, passengers will be treated to this panoramic view of the settlement and the entire northern coast of Molokai's "backside."

▶

All alone on an Easter Sunday morning as the sounds of day awaken with the first rays of light approaching Kalaupapa from the Island of Maui to the east.

▲ Much of Molokai's game management areas are open for pig, goat, and deer hunting year 'round. A Hawaii hunting license is required; a map of the area and a good set of lungs come in handy. Although game is abundant, the hunt is a tough one, with heat, jagged rocks and thick foliage to contend with in every direction.

▲ A prime example of deer country near Red Hill in central Molokai. The barren kiawe tree was brought to Hawaii in 1828 from France. Its chief use was the forestation of wasteland. Nectar on the flowers is collected by honey bees, the gummy pods are good cattle and deer fodder, and its limbs are used for fence posts and fuel for the imus (underground ovens). But gee whiz, are their sharp thorns treacherous!

▲ This is a fine specimen of a male Axis deer. All bucks grow the same shaped 6-point antlers and since there are no seasons in Hawaii, they shed their antlers at various times of the year. Their average weight is 150 pounds, and they are extremely wary. Unlike the many other species of deer, the white spots on their hide do not disappear with time, but remain for life.

▶

Bagging himself a fine eating-size wild boar, this hunter now has the hard work of packing it out to the jeep. Most boar hunting is done with the help of specially bred pig dogs used as trackers and grabbers. Often a skilled hunter will use only his sharp knife to dispatch the pig in very close and dangerous quarters.

◄ A mongoose and a seaman's face, cleverly carved into the trunk of this huge eucalyptus tree, is described by the woodcarver as "living art," which forever remains, but ages as the tree continues to grow.

▲ Growing wild along a jeep trail in Molokai's wet forest region, these yellow ginger plants can reach upward to a height of ten or more feet. Their scent is sweetly potent and just a few flowers will fill an entire room with a delightful fragrance.

▲ A woodsman pauses for a short break during laundry day at his mountain cabin deep in the heart of Molokai's forest.

This narrow one-lane jeep trail leads upwards into the very heartland of the Molokai Forest Preserve, a lush rain forest from which Molokai draws most of its water. Because of the enormous amount of deforestation that occurred in the previous century with the cutting of immense areas of valuable sandalwood, large tracks of surrounding mountain areas near here were replanted in the 1920's with various types of trees. This was done to provide additional watershed to the area. Today this mountain region is so thickly covered with various evergreen-type trees that in many places the sun's rays fail to penetrate to the forest floor below.

▲ The Sandalwood Pit is a hand-dug trench 110 feet long, 40 feet wide, and 7 feet deep with sloping sides, resembling the cargo hold of old whaling ships in the early 1800's. It was used as a measure by Hawaiians of how much valuable sandalwood was to be cut before transporting it on their backs to the waiting ships miles away. So many of these precious trees were cut during those days that the large stands of sandalwood now only exist in the history books.

◄

As the road continues toward the Kamakou Preserve, the heavily timbered area gives way to a thicker and lower type of growth that heralds the entrance to a dense rain forest. The unequaled profusion of diverse fern and plant life in every direction almost defies description as each one struggles with its neighbor for the best location to receive the maximum amount of moisture, sunlight and nutrients. It is best to visit here on a dry day and with a 4-wheel drive vehicle.

◄

One of the most colorful and attractive types of bamboo is this wild, variegated, golden-stemmed species. Native to India and Indonesia, this variety is probably Hawaii's most often used ornamental bamboo. Left alone and unattended, it often reaches heights of 50 feet or more.

▲ With frequent periods of heavy rainfall, interrupted by thick, fog-like mists and the lack of adequate sunlight, the forest presents a haven for dense tangles of vegetation and rotting logs to which epiphytes abundantly grow, such as they do here on this dead, hollow tree stump.

▲ On most days, Waikolu Lookout, with its open view to the North Shore, is not very sunny. Its top ridge line that is visible now normally lies hidden from sight by low-lying clouds, and the lines void of vegetation on the canyon walls are filled with countless waterfalls.

▶ Beginning as small raindrops within the higher reaches of the forest, this clear and icy cold mountain stream spirals and twists its way between the valley walls on its way to the open ocean far below.

▲ From high above within the timberland, a winter sun sets into a distant and peaceful Pacific Ocean.

CHAPTER 3 · SOUTH SHORE

▼▼▼▼▼▼▼▼▼▼▼▼▼▼▼▼▼▼▼▼▼▼▼▼▼

Molokai's South Shore is a broad expanse of land ranging from the parched, unsettled and windless southwestern tip to the island's only major town, mid-way along the island's southern coastline.

To the southwest, the terrain steeply descends from the western mountain range to the ocean some 1,200 feet below. As the tradewinds sweep across the upper plains in their horizontal direction, they create a doldrum effect to the south along the base of the mountain, near the ocean. Settled infrequently in the past, a considerable amount of this dusty, dry land today is owned by Molokai Ranch, and their permission must be secured before entering the district.

Traveling east, the mountain range gradually descends to merge with the slightly ascending area of central Molokai. Approaching Kaunakakai, habitation becomes increasingly evident as houses and churches begin to make appearances along both sides of the two-lane road that leads into town.

Settlement in the small town, referred to by some as "K'Kai," is divided into three mini-districts: the town itself with its stores and older residential houses along side streets, a small subdivi-sion on its western side locally known as Manila Camp, and a higher section to the east, referred to as Ranch Camp.

A short distance from the center of town is Molokai's most important lifeline to the rest of Hawaii, the Kaunakakai Harbor. The twice-a-week tug and barge service brings to Molokai most of the essential items used in everyday life, even the fuel to power its electric plant.

Kaunakakai is best described as a town used for daylight activities, and being family oriented, most residents, including merchants, are home for dinner by sunset. The only exception are those few who venture out to pick up some last minute necessities before the town shuts down for the night.

To walk end to end of town takes about five minutes. It is a unique experience to visit some of the stores and poke around for a while. There will be none of the fancy aisles, mass merchandising, or "Blue Light Specials" found in big city stores. You will find the true "mom and pop" stores from a generation or two ago. Shopping is unhurried on Molokai, and people actually have time to chat with one another whether they are friends or strangers.

One of the first sights to greet visitors driving toward Kaunakakai from the airport is this open stretch of road with its view of Kalohi Channel and the Island of Lanai in the distant background.

Reached by four-wheel drive on private land, the salt flats of Palaau are a low-lying region near the ocean, where sea water has evaporated, leaving a deposit of salt over the earth. The shoreline and ocean are beyond the trees in the distance.

Because of the poor condition of the roads and the distance from their fields, Libby Pineapple Company in the 1920's cut a deep channel through the southern shallow reef. Next to this waterway, they constructed a wooden structure called Kolo Wharf, to haul and receive their supplies. When Libby phased out its pineapple production on Molokai, the wharf was abandoned and subsequently was entirely destroyed by fire, with the exception of its water-soaked wooden pilings.

▲ The stillness and luminous reflections of this quiet pond stirs a desire to be in an old wooden row boat with a straw hat and bamboo pole, daydreaming life away within the lush surroundings of the mangrove.

▲ The Oriental mangrove trees, which grow in salt water, were introduced to Molokai to stabilize erosion along the southern shores. It is an efficient soil builder, trapping leaves and debris within its root system, thereby creating muddy, flat land. In the past its limbs were used to make hunting bows and the leaves and roots for special medicines.

A plumeria farm near Kaunakakai commercially grows and exports the plumeria flower to the florist trade throughout the state. The delicately fragranced yellow and white plumeria is one of the most common types of flowers for stringing leis in Hawaii.

The beautiful Rose Plumeria is not used as frequently in lei making because its fragrance is not as concentrated as other varieties. Its wide color range extends from light pink to a deep, dark burgundy.

▲ Kapuaiwa Grove, commonly called "Coconut Grove" near Kaunakakai, was planted by King Kamehameha V in the 1860's. The grove is fed by a cool, fresh water underground stream that flows from the mountains miles away. If you visit here, be careful of falling coconuts from the treetops high above.

▲ At Coconut Grove this old military bunker is left from the days when the U.S. was at war with Japan. Notice the amount of sand erosion that has occurred since the steel and concrete structure was built.

▲ When the waters of the reef are too shallow for the boat's engine to be run, a long slender limb of the mangrove, shown standing upright here near the bow, is used to pole the flat-bottomed vessel over the reef. The water where this boat is resting is only several inches deep.

► This mountain-fed stream flows under the last bridge to be crossed before entering Kaunakakai. Sometimes the winter rains bring flash floods that raise the water level a foot or more above the bridge, requiring a complete halt to traffic flow in both east and west directions.

Experimental corn is grown in small plots on a large scale year 'round on Molokai. The object of this production is to develop corn that has more sweetness, larger kernel, and an overall greater yield.

Near Kaunakakai Harbor is the foundation of what was once King Kamehameha V's summer home during the late 19th Century. Notice the small salt deposit in the red dirt. This entire area is only several feet above sea level.

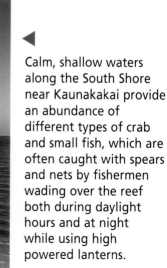

Calm, shallow waters along the South Shore near Kaunakakai provide an abundance of different types of crab and small fish, which are often caught with spears and nets by fishermen wading over the reef both during daylight hours and at night while using high powered lanterns.

▲ Just a few of Molokai's many flat-bottom boats. These homemade vessels are built with their bottom hulls completely flat so that they can be operated in the protected waters of Molokai reefs along the South Shore. They are seldom used, however, in the rough open ocean beyond the reef.

A group of local fishermen harvesting their "lay net" (gill net) on the shallow reef at low tide. ▶

▶ Near Kaunakakai, dusk turns the sky golden as night descends, flooding the flat bottom fleet with waves of glowing warmth.

▲ Looking westward toward the Palaau Salt Flats and Hale O Lono Harbor, the sky offers a beautiful display of cumulus and stratus clouds as they lazily drift by in a southwesterly direction.

▲ Completely underwater most of the time, these lava boulders covered with mossy seaweed lay dry and exposed for only brief periods of time each day when the tide is low. This variety is not the edible type and is extremely slippery for the unwary when stepped upon.

▲ Kaunakakai Wharf, extending seaward almost 1/2 mile, is used for the docking and warehousing of inventory. It also provides a sheltered mooring for a number of commercial fishing vessels and private boats, powered by either sail or engine.

An ocean-going tug with its barge of goods heading into Kaunakakai Harbor provides Molokai's most important link to the rest of Hawaii. Twice a week it provides such items as fresh milk, furniture, gasoline, automobiles and other items that are necessary in everyday life on the island. ►

◄ A small, trim and well-kept wooden sailboat sits safely in the calm waters of its mooring at the harbor. Here it is well protected from the strong northeast trade winds that continually blow across these waters much of the year.

◄ Peddling their way to their favorite spot on the wharf, this group of fine, young fishermen are headed for a day of fun in the sun. During the summer and on most weekends, a large number of the local children can be found enjoying themselves with water activities or simply passing the time away.

Terry Lowry

Terry Lowry

◄ The Scrawled Filefish is a reef dweller and is closely related to the triggerfish family. It has iridescent blue markings scattered over its brown skin and is found throughout the Hawaiian Island chain in the coral-rimmed coastal areas.

▲ One of the most beautiful reef species well-known to aquarium enthusiasts, a Moorish Idol slowly swims by, feeding with its long snout, as a large school of practically motionless goatfish hover in the background.

▲ When the halalu (young mackerel or akule) have their run in the fall of each year, much of the island's population will hurry down to Kaunakakai Harbor with bamboo poles and hooks so small that only a youthful eye can thread a line on to them. When fishing is good, it is not uncommon to catch a 5 gallon bucket full of these small fish, while having 50 barrels of laughs!

These five friends are enjoying a great day exploring among the rocks and coral below the walkway to the boats. Who knows what treasures lay hidden under the next stone as they search for small crabs and fish among the rocks. ▶

▶ When all of that adventure gets the best of them, there is always time to take a plunge and go for a swim in the cool ocean. After all, that is what these hot summer days are made for!

▲ There are plenty of "shaka" signs from these guys, showing their approval of the water's temperature and the time well spent enjoying this fine summer day.

▲ No room for people here. After a gill net is harvested from the ocean, it is sometimes so completely packed full of fish that it must be placed into a smaller vacant boat and towed back to shore by a larger flat-bottomed vessel.

▲ Both skipper and crew of this charter boat have a reason to grin with a nice marlin the size of this one. The fish will be cut up into steak-size fillets and sold to local markets and restaurants. If you have not eaten fresh caught marlin, you've missed a great meal!

Armed with a heavy rod and reel, this shore fisherman has his reward for spending a cold, lonely night on a rocky beach - a 65-pound catch. The ulua, or giant trevally, is a highly prized game fish in Hawaii, growing to over 5 feet and 200 pounds. It is a favored catch of shore fishermen. Notice the footwear this man has on, called tabis or reef walkers. Because of their surefootedness, these "shoes" are used by locals for hiking and around the slippery beach rocks.

▲ Barely visible, a fishing boat returns to home port with its catch for the day just as the sun kisses the ocean a warm and peaceful good night.

▲ This young lady with her bright smile has had a wonderful time and abundant catch, fishing with her dad in the deep waters of Kalohi Channel off Molokai's southern shore. The fish is mahimahi, one of the best-known and enjoyed Hawaiian fish at the dinner table.

▶ Reaping the reward of a night's "lay-net" fishing, this entire family and many of their friends pitch in a helping hand to get the fish out of the net and quickly packed in ice.

▲ Obviously happy, this young girl is enjoying herself taking the entangled fish from the net, knowing too well that there will be lots of fresh fish for supper tonight.

▶ With their fish to sell, all that these people need is a cooler with ice, a scale, the back of a pickup truck, and a place to park on the main street in Kaunakakai. The word of fresh fish for sale spreads rapidly throughout town, and within an hour or so, their coolers are empty.

▲ Making a left turn off of Highway 460, the only road that extends from the West End to the East End of the island, you enter the town of Kaunakakai, the island's center for activities. Within this first block are located the banks, library, several small shops and the State Office Building.

▲ Rounding the turn of Ala Malama Street, one enters the main drag of Kaunakakai. There are only two short blocks of town, which somewhat resembles a border town in an old Clint Eastwood western movie. This is where the action is! Most of the island's shopping is done here, as is catching up on all of the local news, which in Hawaii is referred to as "talking story."

Located at the easternmost end of Kaunakakai is the Molokai Veterans War Memorial. Near here you will find the fire and police stations, post office, hospital and county offices, where you can secure camping permits. Also in this general area are several baseball fields, where a good local home town game can be found on most summer nights and weekends.

If you need to buy, sell, rent, swap or even want to find someone quickly, the best and cheapest way (free) is to simply write the message on some paper and thumb tack it to one of the town bulletin boards, or "Coconut Wireless."

Local free diver Sammy, with two of his favorite underwater big guns. This sport is not for the timid or weak. The type of fish that is hunted in the swift, deep waters of Molokai often weigh more than a hundred pounds and are full of spirited and savage fight.

▲ Sometimes, you will find young men at a street corner somewhere in town passing idle hours away playing their ukuleles for their own and any passerby's enjoyment.

▲ The participants here are getting ready for the start of the annual Lion's Club Easter Egg Hunt in Kaunakakai. It's hard to believe how fast these kids can run toward those eggs once the signal to start is given. Especially enjoyable are the younger ones with their parents at their very first hunt. They are not quite sure what to do or how to go about it.

▲ "Talking story" is part of the everyday life on Molokai. These people are having a lengthy discussion about the price to be paid per pound for some wild bananas that one man has brought into town from Molokai's tropical east end.

▶ On Molokai, the back yards of most homes have a wide variety of tropical plants that are grown quite easily the entire year 'round. This man brings young plants he has grown in old coffee cans to a local farmer's market every month to sell or trade for varieties which he does not have.

▲ This "to the point" sign made of butcher's paper hangs on a local restaurant's window to advertise its daily lunch special to people walking by in plain and simple pidgin English.

◄

This little piggy went to market! The author took this picture just after the orphaned little piglet was seen running and squealing down the town sidewalk after his adopted mom. It seems she was carrying his baby bottle full of fortified milk and he wanted it, <u>badly!</u>

Selling homemade barbecue chicken, rice cakes and other unusual foods from the back of a station wagon, this lady can be found in town on certain days, as she has been for decades. In several short hours, everything she has cooked for that day is rapidly bought up by the town people.

▼

▶ Going shopping in Kaunakakai is always lots of fun for all. Although the town is small, most stores carry a wide variety of different items. The local shoppers are never in a hurry and most of the time, you can find the most unexpected items in the most unusual places.

Flower leis are used in Hawaii for all special occasions. Just about any type of flower or berry can be used or combined together, the only limit being one's imagination. To make a lei, a special needle from 12 to 18 inches is used. The flowers are threaded on the needle and then are pulled through to the string that holds them in place.

▼

▲ The annual Aloha Week Parade is an island-wide event every October that passes though the main street of Kaunakakai. It is looked forward to, as are all parades, with an air of excitement for the participants as well as everyone along the road side.

▲ This small parade is open to anyone who wants to dress up their truck, scooter, lawn mower or trailer with a little help from friends and lots of wild flowers and plants. This is the result. "Keiki" in the Hawaiian language means child.

▲ Youngsters on the floats have a great time and lots of fun waving to everyone they know, which on Molokai is just about everyone lining both sides of the street.

Every major Island in Hawaii is represented in the parade by lady pa'u (a type of long, flowing skirt) riders and her court, each mounted on a horse behind her. There are eight different groups of riders which represent the eight major islands of Hawaii. Each group of riders wears the color that represents its own island. The purple here exemplifies the Island of Kauai.

▲ Wearing the colors of a pink rose, this pa`u rider is representative of the Island of Maui. In Hawaii leis are not only worn around the shoulders. There are hat and head leis for both men and women, and even horse leis made from combining flowers, berries and foliage.

Representing the Island of Oahu, this court rider is wearing yellow and gives a local "shaka" sign, which to locals has a variety of meanings, depending on the circumstance, such as "How's it?" or "Everything is o.k."

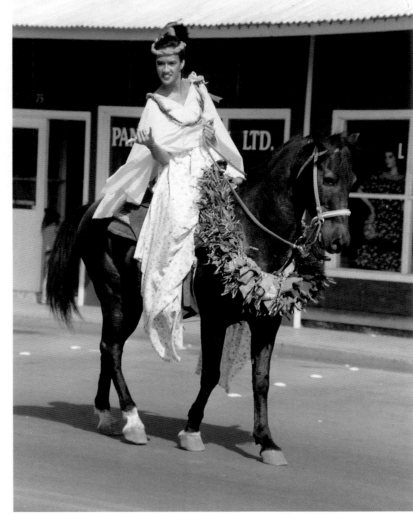

Running across a field of flowers, a wooden deer leads the way atop this float. "E Pili Mai" in Hawaiian means "to come together as one."

◀

For the young, a parade is something new and exciting to behold. It fills their eyes and minds with dreams of fantasies and wonderment.

At the other end of the scale, where ever you can find a bench or resting place, you will normally find a group of old timers talking, thinking, watching and just passing time in their golden years as the rest of town goes about the business of its daily life.

▼

▲ Horses were first brought to Hawaii in 1803 from California. The paniolo, or cowboy, evolved as a result of three Mexican cowboys being invited to the Big Island of Hawaii in 1832 to teach the Hawaiians how to ride and rope. Horses are used far and wide on Molokai for jobs 4-wheel drive vehicles are not capable of doing. This paniolo wears a hat lei of kukui leaves, the official tree of Molokai.

▶

After a parade and on most summer holidays, you can find Molokai's paniolos down at the rodeo arena testing their skills along with horsemen that periodically visit from neighboring islands.

◀ If Molokai had one sport, it would be baseball. Here the teams, men and women, young and old, play baseball 52 weeks a year among themselves and in tournaments that bring teams to the island from all over Hawaii. Although always played with good-natured fun, the game is taken very seriously by the opposing teams.

◀ The author watched this young boy for 5 minutes trying to get the little girl to give him a bite of her apple. He must have done or said something right, because she finally handed it over to him.

▲ On the sideline, these two young girls are enjoying cheering and giving support to their favorite team. The smaller one looks like she has already mastered the art of making a "shaka" sign.

▲ In the days of ancient Hawaiians, the Makahiki season was a period of four months set aside for peace and love in honor of the god Lono. During this time, war ceased and games of skill and expertise took its place. It was a time of Lokahi, a time for the community to come together in unity and harmony. On Molokai every year, the tradition continues on a designated weekend with many of the same games of the olden days being played among the school children from the different districts of Molokai.

▲ There are many different types of sports played at the Makahiki. These two children are engaged in Hakoko Moa, a form of one-legged wrestling, the object of which is to knock the opponent down or push him outside of the ring while the victor still remains standing on one leg.

◄

A member of the fig family, the banyan tree is a very large and slow-growing tree that originally came from India and China. Aerial roots grow along its outer limbs and anchor themselves securely to the earth, allowing the tree to continue to grow outward, covering a sizeable area. It is not uncommon for a banyan to cover an entire block. Pictured here is a Chinese banyan, which has fewer auxiliary trunks and more of a ribbed appearance than the Indian variety.

Called Flame of the Forest, the African Tulip tree produces a variety of brilliantly colored orange-red flowers that can be seen from great distances surrounded by the otherwise green landscape. Originally discovered in Africa in the 1700's, the tree can be found growing wild throughout Molokai. Note the mynah bird high above, feeding among the flowering buds.

▼

▶

A coconut tree will bear up to 200 coconuts a year and live 75 years. In populated areas, agile men climb the trees regularly to cut young coconuts before they can ripen and fall to the ground, possibly injuring someone.

Not only used for their meat and milk, coconut trees yield tough but pliable leaves that skilled local men and women weave into durable hats to provide a bit of shade from the hot Hawaiian sun.

▼

◄

This Guatemalan avocado tree is native to Mexico and Central America. The skin of the fruit is usually thick, woody and rough. It matures during the spring and summer months, and it is common to find an avocado weighing as much as a pound or more. The local population calls this variety a "butter avocado" because of its rich texture.

◄

Mango is one of the finest and best known tropical fruits and is sometimes called the "King of Fruits." Native to India, it was introduced to Hawaii sometime after 1800. The mango grows abundantly on Molokai, with trees reaching a height of 70 feet, covered with a heavy luxuriant foliage. There are many different varieties of these trees, each producing a fruit of different size and sweetness.

◄

Just about every weekend these Homestead farmers sell truckloads of papayas in Kaunakakai. Eaten ripe for breakfast or for dessert, the fruit may also be cooked green with chicken or meats. In addition, the peppery seeds are used to make salad dressing.

▶

Eighty-pound stalks of bananas are quite easily grown in any back yard on Molokai. Once a stalk of bananas is harvested, the entire tree must be cut down, as it will no longer bear fruit. Suckers that sprout around the older tree's base will produce several new trees, which in turn will produce fruit only once during its lifetime.

Cock fighting is illegal on Molokai and throughout Hawaii. However, game cocks are often bred for show and "sparring" in some local backyards. Because of the aggressive behavior of the cocks toward others of their own kind, each rooster is tethered and lives separately, out of striking distance from the neighboring bird.

▼

▲ Although Molokai's population is mostly Polynesian, with the highest percentage of Hawaiian blood in the state, there is also a small number of Caucasians, both young and old, who have settled quite happily into the simple and rural lifestyle. Here are two of them that seem to be pondering the higher meaning of their existence over a can of cold beer.

◀

"Please remove shoes before entering" is a custom that is very common throughout the State of Hawaii and should be respected when visiting another's home or abode.

▲ Training for the hula starts at an early age for young island girls. Here is a one-year-old all dressed up in her new birthday outfit. As the well-known Hawaiian song goes, "Keep your eyes on the hands..."

▲ Authentic Hawaiian luaus are far different from those portrayed in the resort areas throughout the state, as people sip their Mai Tais and watch Tahitian dancers. True luaus are held in both parks and family back yards and the dress is always informal: rubber slippers, T shirts and shorts are the norm. It is a time to visit with acquaintances and relatives, check out that friend's new baby you haven't seen, drink a little Budweiser, and listen to some good Hawaiian music, usually played by someone's relative.

▲ With the open ocean as a backdrop and the tradewinds for an air conditioner, bands such as this, made up of both local men and women, provide the music to keep a luau flowing with entertainment.

▲ It is a tradition in Hawaii to have a birthday luau for a child when they reach their first birthday. The event is a celebration for the entire family, including toddlers as well as grandparents. Those attending bring gifts in addition to well-wishes. The little boy in the white tux, with his Tongan grandfather holding him, is guest of honor at this party.

▲ The brilliance of Molokai's sunsets are truly unforgettable. In the foreground, a family has embedded a Christmas tree into the reef in a gesture that would seem to echo a message to reach all lands across the sea at this special time of the year: "Peace on Earth."

CHAPTER 4 · EAST END

▼▼▼▼▼▼▼▼▼▼▼▼▼▼▼▼▼▼▼▼

Almost a half million years after the formation of the parched flatlands of western Molokai, another much more powerful volcano on the ocean's floor pushed upwards and created the high steep mountain range of Molokai's East End. The loftiness of this range is sufficient enough to trap wind and cloud movements that bring along with them heavy rainfall that descends upon the entire region.

Abundant rains have in turn cut river valleys which carved the aged volcanic lands into intricate troughs and ridges. Down these rocky river beds, a flood of minerals came to settle along the coastal lands and created a dark rich soil that is ideal for agriculture. The surrounding calm, protected and shallow reefs, as well as fertile deep water fishing grounds, host an abundant supply of food to harvest from the sea. All combined, these elements lead to a healthy, established society that has existed along the southeastern coastal zone for decades.

Still visible today along the seashores and inland areas are ancient fish ponds once used for aquaculture, terraces for agriculture, and heiaus for worship. Because of these rich resources, the old inhabitants of Molokai were considered very wealthy. As a result of needing to protect their wealth, they became fierce and mighty warriors, dreaded throughout the Hawaiian Island chain. Feared not only for their might in battle, they also developed over time into an even more powerful and revered family of priests and sorcerers, called kahunas.

Presently, this thick and lush district, showered by constant tropical rains, is settled by local families who have lived there for generations in a simple way, close to their aina (land). Many grow taro and other fruits and vegetables on small pieces of land near their home. They hunt wild pig, goat and deer deep in the valleys and high on the mountains. From the ocean, they harvest fish with spears and nets as their ancestors did before them. It is a hard and simple life, but extremely rewarding.

Development is slow to come to Molokai and even slower to the East End. Along with the rustic and sparsely populated community, some newer homes have sprung up near the ocean and on the hillsides. There is one condominium complex, located near Mile Marker 13, which houses local residents and accommodates visitors.

Beautiful white sand coves lace the coastline along the narrow, and at times, one-lane road which leads through the district. The most spectacular snorkeling on all of Molokai can be found along this isolated passage that eventually winds through a stunning 14,000-acre private ranch, and then down into the depths of Halawa itself.

The remains of an ancient fishpond located along Molokai's southeastern shore.

▲ The Kakahaia National Wildlife Refuge, with its 15-acre freshwater pond and its surrounding 42 acres of land, is home for a dozen species of sea and coastal birds. This area, called Kawela, was once a City of Refuge in the days of the early Hawaiians. Such a refuge was a place where a person who committed a crime would be safe from persecution if they reached its designated boundary before being captured.

▲ Five miles east of Kaunakakai is this pleasant day park. It's an enjoyable place to stop for a cookout and picnic, or simply to walk along the sandy beach. Overnight camping, however, is not permitted.

▲ The Pakuhiwa Battlegrounds along the seashore near Kawela was the site of two great battles, fought between Kamehameha the Great and the rulers of Molokai during Kamehameha's quest to unite all of the islands under his rule. Beyond in the distance is the stormy, white-capped Kalohi Channel and the Island of Lanai. Molokai's protected coral reefs and sandy channels which span its southern shore can be clearly seen.

▲ Evening descends on Molokai's southeastern shore without so much as a ripple on the ocean which would betray the passing of citizens living near its mirrored surface.

▶

Looking northeastward while traveling towards Halawa Valley, the mountains abruptly begin their ascent a short distance away from the narrow flat coastal zone. Known as Kamakou, this primitive, harsh and uninhabited mountain range rises upward to a height of almost 5,000 feet and divides Molokai's northern and southern shores. Throughout this largely inaccessible and roadless area there are abundant herds of wild goats, Axis deer, boar and exotic game birds. For the hunter that ventures onto its steep slopes and into its canyons, or the occasional hiker that explores this incredible vastness of nature, the upper heights beholds a vista with absolute magnificence!

▼

▲ Founded and personally built in 1876 by Father Damien, the small and quaint St. Joseph's Church stands quietly along the roadside 11 miles east of Kaunakakai.

▲ Although the front door of the church remains closed, it is unlocked for those wishing to visit inside. A small box within will accept donations for the upkeep of the church.

▶

A statue of Father Damien DeVeuster, clad in a cape with his cane, graces the yard next to a small cemetery outside St. Joseph's Catholic Church. He is often remembered as the "Martyr of Molokai" because of his tireless efforts to improve the well-being of those inflicted with leprosy and exiled to the Kalaupapa Peninsula in the late 1800's. Father Damien himself died from complications of leprosy after having served sixteen years to those suffering from the dreaded disease.

◀

These two horses on Molokai enjoy a free and healthy life, grazing in lush pastures and always getting plenty of exercise. However, they seem to be having the same thoughts as most people - the grass always looks greener on the other side of the fence.

◀

At this spot in 1927, Ernest Smith and Emory Bronte safely crash landed their plane after having made the first civilian transpacific flight, which lasted in excess of 25 hours. In that day and age, they were extremely lucky to have been within reach of level ground after having made a flight of such a long distance.

◀

Cultivation of this lowland (wet) taro requires construction of ditches, bringing water from streams to flood the banked rows of the taro patch. Taro was the most important crop of the ancient Hawaiians. Its root (called a corm) is still used today in the making of poi, taro chips or steamed like a potato.

Our Lady of Sorrows Catholic Church was built by Father Damien in 1874 in his efforts to convert the people of Molokai to Christianity. It was the first Catholic church on Molokai outside of the Kalaupapa settlement.

Countless years of rainfall have eroded the southeastern face of Molokai into numerous V-shaped canyons. Heavier rainfall on the north or windward side have formed broad cavernous valleys whose walls are so steep it is difficult to reach the northern coast from the summit region. While driving along the coastal road after rains in the mountains above, huge waterfalls can be seen, plunging downward hundreds of feet among the walls of the many canyons throughout this area.

▲ In the early 1900's Ah Ping Store was once a gathering place for the local East End residents, as well as the only gas pump east of Kaunakakai. Although unused for many years, the yard is always cut and trimmed, as if the store were still open, pumping gasoline and the shelves stocked with goods.

▲ What memories must be stored within this broken and rusty hulk - weekly trips to town, the family's Sunday drives, and perhaps a young person's first attempt at driving under the watchful eye of their parent sitting next to him.

A small mountain stream flows silently under one of the many bridges on the eastern side of the island. During some periods of heavy rain, flash floods occur, expanding the rivers, covering nearby yards with several inches of water and halting traffic along the only road in the district.

The American and Hawaiian flags proudly fly in the northeastern tradewinds in a yard on the East End. The Hawaiian flag is a combination of the British Union Jack and the American Stars and Stripes.

◄

In the ancient days, Molokai was known and respected for her religious mastery. Throughout the island there are many remains of heiaus, or temples, but none as impressive as Iliiliopae, the largest, and said to be the oldest. It was a powerful temple of the highest order and was known to be a place of human sacrifice. Pictured is the extremely level main platform, which on its eastern end is 22 feet above ground and sloping to 11 feet on its western side.

◄

At the eastern end of the heiau there are terraces which lead to the main platform. To build Iliiliopae it is said that water-worn stones were carried and passed hand to hand in a human chain over the Wailau Trail, which begins just behind the heiau. The path ascends to a height of 2,800 feet before descending steeply into Wailau Valley, some 8 miles away.

◄

A short distance up the Wailau Trail, the massive size of the temple becomes apparent by viewing two-thirds of the main platform's 286 foot length and 87 foot width. Building this heiau was a feat of gigantic proportions, considering thousands upon thousands of stones were laid by hand, without the use of mortar.

▶ Hawaiians of old had no written language. Their history, folklore, learning and genealogies were passed on from one generation to the next in the form of chants or stories. Chanting is still practiced by men and women today who have spent a lifetime learning about their heritage, and in turn they pass it down in this manner to the younger generation.

Even an overgrown and thorny thicket of kiawe trees can become a beautiful and serene place to catch one of Molokai's peaceful sunsets. It is said that if there are no clouds on the horizon and you are lucky, the sun will flicker a brilliant green flash just before it disappears.

▼

◀

Throughout much of Molokai, often a narrow winding dirt road through a thick maze of tropical vegetation will lead to someone's very private and hidden front yard. So remote are some of these houses that they are still without the everyday comforts, such as telephones and electricity.

Near Mile Marker 17, the East End's large amount of heavy rainfall becomes apparent by the abundant green foliage that literally seems to reach for the sky as it completely covers small trees, the ground, and anything within its ever-grasping reach.

▼

▲ A small wooden farm house, nestled comfortably at the base of these green hills, seems to breathe tranquility with a sense of well-being. The amount of green encompassing this area leaves the eyes simply amazed.

► With no explanation needed, this cozy and useful little throne combines all the comforts of indoor plumbing with a panoramic outdoor view.

◀ Tossed and carried by the currents, this weathered tree root finds a resting place among the shore-lined lava rocks. Often during winter storms, entire trees will land on shore, pushed by currents from as far away as the West Coast of the United States.

▲ Along the southeastern shores of Molokai are located the largest amount of fish ponds, built during the ancient times in Hawaii. Constructed of stone and coral, the commoners used them to raise and fatten fish for royalty's use. The remnants of one is pictured here.

▲ A perfect day's end on the beach at a rustic fisherman's hut. The simple beauty of such places as this can be found at many locations, from Kaunakakai Town to the far reaches of the East End.

▲ Though seldom seen in Molokai waters by skin divers, this 6 foot reef shark, with hook and line still attached, was caught by a shore fisherman that was in search of a much better table fare.

▶ Leisurely winding its way up a speed limit sign, this creeping vine is very symbolic in regard to driving on the narrow, bending roads on the east end toward Halawa Valley...you must go slowly.

▲ Destroyed by fire a century ago, this solitary rock stack, located near Mile Marker 20, is all that remains of Molokai's first sugar mill.

◄

Places such as this shallow reef area are excellent for gathering limu (edible seaweed). The limit is one pound per day, and it is against the law to take the holdfast (the part attached to the rocks) or to take it when it is covered with reproductive nodes. Only certain types are edible and preparation is required, so be sure you know what to do before picking.

The most widely used snorkeling spot on Molokai for locals and visitors alike is at Mile Marker 20, east of Kaunakakai. It is a nice, calm area that provides a pleasant place for kids and adults to enjoy a day of water activities. On certain days, the shallow reef's water is so clear that all of the coral heads and many tropical fish can be seen from above the water.

▼

Terry Lowry

▲ This White Spotted Toby is of the Puffer fish family. When frightened, it is capable of inflooding its body with water to a much larger than normal size, in an effort to frighten and make it difficult for predators to swallow.

▶

Terry Lowry

The Ornate Butterfly fish usually swim in pairs. Being a coral feeder, they can normally be found in areas where there is an abundance of reef to feed upon.

▶

A small and secluded spot that is perfect for the children to play while mom watches and dad does some rod fishing from the boulders into the deep waters of the bay. Spear fishing is excellent here as well, but beware of currents on the frequently windy days.

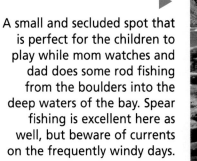

◄ Just beyond Mile Marker 20, this lava rock outcropping offers a good foothold for casting your fishing line into deep water where some of Hawaii's larger game fish lurk. Keep a watchful eye for green sea turtles drifting about, and during the winter months, look for the many great whales that migrate here each year to give birth to their calves. At times the whales can be seen breaching completely out of the water, other times swimming lazily by in small groups feeding in the rich waters offshore.

◄ The silvery Beach Heliotrope grows throughout Hawaii, seemingly without soil, on barren lava rocks within reach of salty spray. A related succulent plant with pink flowers, Tetramolopium Rockii, is found only on Molokai.

▲ With some skill and luck, this fisherman will have a good-size fish in his ice chest today, and an even bigger-sized story to talk about tomorrow.

▶ When standing near the water's edge, always be aware of the ocean's swells as they reach the beach or rocks. Often the power of these waves can be under-estimated, resulting in the very least a set of wet clothes.

In spite of the fact that his fishing line has become a bit tangled up, this young local boy is still enjoying his day at the beach. Fishing is an integral part of life on Molokai, and children learn the fundamentals starting at an early age.

▼

Terry Lowry

Terry Lowry

▲ Cauliflower coral is usually found in shallow waters that are exposed to wave action. Commonly found on Molokai, it is a safe haven and home for many species of small fish, crab and shellfish that hide within its folds. It is unlawful to intentionally take or damage any live stony coral throughout the State of Hawaii.

▲ Ascending to the surface above, this scuba diver gives the Hawaiian "shaka" sign to his dive buddy, indicating everything is all right. During snorkeling, as well as scuba diving, it is always best to have a companion go along.

▶

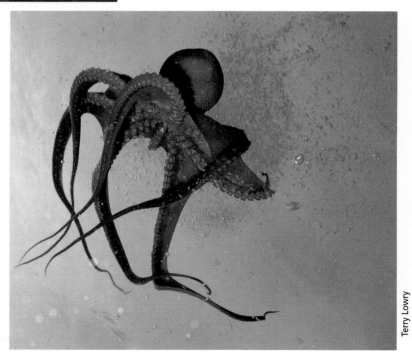

Octopus, or he'e as it is called in Hawaii, is a shy creature that can be found in numbers along most of Molokai's southern and eastern shores. Since they are boneless except for their strong beak, which can inflict a painful bite, they are able to squeeze into hiding places many times smaller than their normal size. They feed on smaller crab, mollusks and shrimp.

Terry Lowry

▲ Called Sandy Beach, this cozy little cove offers a bit of something for everyone as they have fun in the sun. The crystal-clear light green water beckons divers to explore the small colorful reef just footsteps away from the sand.

▲ Clearly visible are the varying depths and spectacular coral heads at Honouliwai Bay. There is usually good fishing to be had where the reef drops off into a deeper shade of blue. Local fishermen also anchor their boats inside the bay, using the natural channel to venture in and out.

◄ Commonly known as Rock Point, this lava formation on the oceanside of the road heading east is a well-known landmark for the local surfers and boogie boarders that converge here when the surf is up.

Terry Lowry

◄ Butterfly fish are known for their brilliant colors arranged in bold patterns, one of their most outstanding features. They live together in large groups of closely related species in craggy reef areas. Pictured here is the Raccoon Butterfly fish.

▲ Waist deep in the ocean, these men seem to have the right idea: if the fish won't come to you, then you go to the fish.

Terry Lowry

◄ The Boxfish acquired its name because the body is encased in a solid-ridged bony box of hexagonal plates. They are unable to use their bodies for swimming and solely rely on their fins and tail for propulsion, making them extremely slow swimmers.

▲ Named for the trees that surround it, Pine Tree Bluff offers a sweeping, panoramic view of the ocean between the islands of Maui and Molokai, combined with the harsh and jagged land along the coastline. Along the rocky shores of Hawaii, which are continually pounded by the ocean's waves, strong and agile men journey to pick the much sought after limpet called opihi. They often descend cliffs by ropes in order to find the biggest, ranging in size from a quarter to a 50-cent piece. Often selling for as much as $200/gallon, the gathering of this strong-tasting morsel, served at most traditional luaus, is best left to the experienced. Each year in Hawaii some of those who venture after the opihi are swept off the rocks to their death. In the distance is Moku Hooniki Island.

▲ Living on Molokai's East End can best be described as "laid back." There are a scattered number of older residential houses whose families have lived in the same general area for generations. Most shopping is done in Kaunakakai, and the only intermediate and high school is located in Kualapuu, some 28 miles away.

▲ Continuing east, the narrow, winding road that follows the water's edge is one built with a sense of purpose, a slow purpose. There are frequent places along the way to pull over and take a short, exploratory walk and sample the gentle sea breezes.

◀

With the last rays of sunlight, calmness and tranquility settle over Molokai with only an occasional distant laughter from a nearby party to interrupt the endless sound of the ocean washing gently against the sand and rocks.

 A cluster of succulent century plants with their two-foot long pointed leaves flourish on a hardened clay embankment, as the road turns inland along the steep inclines of eastern Molokai.

In this hard and rocky earth, old weathered fence posts made from the kiawe tree seem to take a wandering path to reach an unknown destination in the distance.

▼

◄

Stunning 14,000 acre Puu O Hoku Ranch, located high above the eastern coast, is the largest ranch on this side of the island. The narrow paved road through the property provides the only access into Halawa Valley for residents and visitors.

◄

Moku Hooniki Island and Kanaha Rock, used during World War II for bombing targets, now lie barren, except for the occasional sea birds that visit their lonely, rocky slopes.

◄

Seeing this empty and neglected house one has to stop and wonder what life here must have been like when its wood was new, the roads unpaved, and the only night lights were stars and kerosene lamps.

Beginning the descent into Halawa Valley down the narrow road that is cut into the face of sheer cliffs, the scenery suddenly changes from rolling pastureland to a profuse overgrowth of tropical vegetation, unfolding in every direction.

The Uluhea, a lacelike fern, springs to life from the many soil embankments as the road turns and winds its way ever deeper down the side of the mountain into the depths of the valley.

Not unlike the petroglyphs of ancient times, here modern day travelers have paused long enough to etch a reminder that they, too, have passed this way.

▲ This distant view of Moaula Falls reveals the thick tropical jungle that the traveler will have to hike through during his 1 1/2 hour journey to reach the falls. At least twenty ancient heiau sites have been officially recorded throughout Halawa Valley. Their purposes varied, from agricultural and fishing shrines to places of worship and prayer. Some were dedicated to the shark god and others to the god of fishermen. At least eight have been reported to have been for human sacrifice.

▲ Remote Halawa Valley, thought to have been first settled around 600 A. D., had in the early 1900's a bustling community which was destroyed by a tidal wave in 1946. It now stands empty, except for a few shacks, home to fisherman and farmers, and a small church, nestled quietly among its green surroundings.

The largest stream on Molokai, fed from Hipuapua and Moaula waterfalls high above, carves a winding path that empties into Halawa Bay. During the summer, the bay provides a safe harbor for the few boats that venture to this far end of the island. During the winter's dangerous high surf, boats in this area are virtually nonexistent, and the only activity this solitary retreat experiences is the endless crashing of the ocean upon its shore.

◀ All that remains of the old church with the passage of wind and time are the four massive hand-built walls and the stark openings of its vacant windows and doors.

▲ Built in 1852 of stone, and later plastered with lime, the old Halawa Congregational Church was used up until the late 1940's when a tidal wave hit, destroying much of the community. Many of the inhabitants of the valley were forced to move to other areas of Molokai, and the church fell into neglect.

▲ Giant wild pothos grasps onto anything within its reach and spreads its domain skyward, limited only to the height of its host.

▶

Charming and quaint, this little church, called King of Kings and Lord of Lords, sits peacefully on the floor of Halawa Valley. It occasionally has services for residents and visitors who are passing through, which has been the custom since 1940 when it was built.

Near the mouth of Halawa Bay, huge water-smoothed lava rocks and massive driftwood trees lie tossed upon the shore as if they were mere pebbles and twigs, attesting to the power of the mighty Pacific Ocean during the winter storms.

▼

◀ Setting up an open-air shop on his front porch, it's just another day at the office for this man, selling a few of the necessary items you might find a need for on a visit to Halawa and forgot to buy before leaving Kaunakakai.

▲ Specially designed throw nets are used for catching fish as they swim close to shore. When spotted, the fisherman hurls his net into the rolling surf in hopes of trapping some, if not all, of the passing fish. When tears occur in the net from sharp rocks, it must be repaired using monofilament line and a special needle, as this man is doing.

▲ Giant pothos grow lavishly throughout Halawa Valley and creates a mystical and timeworn feeling. The plant has adapted so incredibly well that it sends down feeder roots as much as 50 feet to the ground to secure its needed nutrients.

▲ Less dense and sunnier areas of the valley take on strange shapes as thick masses of vines and pothos tangle and wind their way around the trees that grow here, completely engulfing them.

▲ The hike to Moaula Falls winds through private property, so be sure to check if the trail is open at one of the visitor information offices before beginning your journey. During the trip to the falls, one stream will have to be crossed. It's not very deep during the dry season; however, the underwater rocks are quite slippery. In periods of heavy rain, exercise caution, as flash floods are known to occur in this area.

▲ Leaving the stream behind and proceeding deeper into the valley, the only sign of man's continued presence is a narrow, footworn path that gives one the feeling they are alone on a great adventure!

▲ Among the many plants you will encounter along the route to the falls, the giant Alocacia reaches higher than a man's head, trying to capture the sun's rays above the darkened floor of the forest.

▲ High above in the canopy of the forest, giant rosettes of bird's nest ferns, with their translucent green leaves, form a magnificent sight among the branches of a sunlit tree.

▲ As Moaula Falls grow nearer, the sound of water tumbling against rock intensifies. The trail weaves away from the stream into the dense foliage, and the stream's elegant song echoes through the forest.

Hala trees had many uses for the people of old Hawaii. The lauhala (leaf of the hala tree) was woven into mats for sleeping, pillows, sandals, and even sails for outrigger canoes. Its hard, red fruit sections were worn as leis by the alii (members of the ruling class). Today, especially prized are lauhala hats, which a vanishing few of the old timers still make. They sell for several hundred dollars and are often topped with hand-made feather leis that can cost as much as one thousand dollars.

Throughout the valley there are still signs of early inhabitants created in stone. Rock walls, terraces, and even house foundations can still be seen, standing in silent testimony of the builder's toils and struggles with life in his tropical paradise.

▲ When Halawa Valley was populated, it contained over one thousand taro patches and supplied much of Molokai's needs. These stone walls were built to protect the cultivated field from roaming animals, as well as to establish boundaries throughout the area.

▲ Along the trail, as well as in many other parts of Molokai, offerings wrapped in ti leaves may be found. They symbolize prayers to the ancient ones who may have passed this way in hopes that they won't become offended by someone treading on their sacred grounds. These natural alms should not be disturbed. Some of the offerings here include awapuhi, a type of ginger that can be used as a shampoo to wash one's hair.

The ninety-minute hike ends abruptly among a mass of huge boulders and a breathtaking view of Moaula Falls. As legend has it, the giant mo`o (lizard) lives beneath this icy pool. Before entering the water, a visitor must drop a single ti leaf on the surface. If it floats, the mo`o will be tolerant of swimmers and one may enter. If the ti leaf sinks, the mo`o's domain is not to be disturbed and danger faces those who challenge his command.

CHAPTER 5 · NORTH SHORE (BACKSIDE)

▼▼▼▼▼▼▼▼▼▼▼▼▼▼▼▼▼▼▼▼▼▼▼▼▼▼▼▼▼▼▼▼

Molokai's remote North Shore is an unspoiled, primitive place that even today remains hidden and lost from the outside world. It is fourteen miles of the most spectacular and isolated land in all the Hawaiian Islands, virtually untouched for decades by human presence. Were it not for the modern airplane and power boat, even fewer people today would have knowledge of the existence of the majestic beauty which lies hidden just around the corner from Halawa Valley.

Practically unsettled for almost one hundred years, this rugged land was once home to a strong and proud people who, for a thousand years, worked their land and fished the sea. Today, stone walls, terraces for cultivating taro, and heiaus lie hidden beneath thickets of bamboo, hala trees, and vegetation that quickly reclaim the land.

Along the imposing cliffs that extend for miles, frequent rainfall high in the forest sends water below to supply the uncountable waterfalls that cascade over the vertical sides and plunge into the ocean far below.

The surrounding ocean abounds, with tuna, mahimahi, huge sea turtles, marlin, lobster, and countless other denizens of the sea, a direct result of the inaccessibility of the North Shore. To these rich waters also the giant humpback whale makes its yearly migration to mate and birth their calves.

The northern coast now is home only to the sure-footed wild goats that scamper along the rocky ledges, the lively black pigs that dart hastily into the bamboo thickets at the first sound of approach, and the many sea birds that soar and dive among the rocky crevices high above. It is truly a flawless and pristine wilderness, where man is now the only intruder.

▲ Approaching Wailau Valley, an unnamed waterfall endlessly carves its path into the face of the northern cliffs as it journeys downward to merge with the blue Pacific far below.

◄

An aerial view reveals how remote and inaccessible Molokai's North Shore is to the outside world. There are no scheduled guided tours of this side of the island. During the calm waters of the summer months, however, it is possible to find an occasional fisherman who is willing to take a few passengers "backside."

◄

Your last view of "civi-lization" will be as you depart the sheltered waters of Halawa Bay by boat for the deep waters of the open ocean and the desolate, alluring backside. Fishermen and campers make up the majority of those who venture to this lonely, untamed coast.

◄

Some locals and their families spend a few days or weeks each year camping in the few isolated areas that are flat enough to set up their tents. All necessary items must be brought with them in waterproof containers. The campers will have to swim to shore with their supplies, since the boat is unable to approach the rocky coast. Here is a group of four heading for a quiet and peaceful week-end near Puahauni Point.

► Once a campsite is selected, the party must remain there until the boat returns on a designated day and time. Traveling to areas other than where they were put ashore is not possible except by swimming, because of the steep, vertical sea cliffs and rocky coastline that best describes 99% of the northern shores.

▲ The sea arch Keanapuka, with Kikipua Point in the distant background. Near this area were built massive stone walls and heiaus, which were dedicated to the ancient shark god and to Kuula, the god of fishermen. There are also platforms and terraces that were used as an advanced school of higher learning, or college, for priests.

► Papalaua Valley is a short box canyon which contains one of the highest and most spectacular waterfalls in the state. It lies almost hidden from view within the steep walls of the valley. Heavy rainfall from high above allows the falls to cascade down the cliff's sides practically every day of the year.

▲ Looking westward from Kikipua Point near the site of the ancient heiaus provides a partial view of the 14 miles of lonely and imposing coastline that is reachable only by helicopter or boat. Along the upper heights of the North Shore, the rainfall is considerable, almost 25 <u>feet</u> a year!

◄

Multitudes of ribbon-like waterfalls thread their way down the face of Lepau Point's sheer cliffs, merging with the salt water below. Near here are the highest sea cliffs in the world, rising in excess of 2,000 feet above the waves that continually wash against its coastal foundation.

▲ The only sandy beach on the backside is that fronting Wailau Valley, which means "many waters." The sand here disappears during the winter storms; however, the summer tides and currents return most which was lost to the coastal shore of the valley. The valley's inhabitants in ancient times were known for making special kapa cloth which was used for covering their idols and another oiled variety which was used in sorcery. It is said that from this area the stones were carried over the high mountains from the North Shore on the Wailau trail, to build Iliiliopae Heiau.

▶

▶

Waiehu Flat is one of the few places along the coast where the towering cliffs do not continue their descent to the ocean floor. In such areas, hala trees and other tropical vegetation form dense and impenetrable growth from the ocean's edge to the vertical cliffs.

▲ Looking west from Kaholaiki Bay. For centuries, the North Shore was settled with scattered villages in and around its valleys. The people were mostly farmers and fishermen who occasionally visited other villages by means of outrigger canoes, to trade and barter their harvest of crops and fish. The valleys were abandoned by the year 1919 because of their isolation and a period of economic stagnation that settled over Molokai, causing its population to drop to 1,117 in 1920.

▲ Pelekunu is a wide and deep valley that cuts almost through the center of Molokai to its southern side. So steep are the vertical walls that its very name when translated into English means "smelly from lack of sunshine." The bay is fed by four streams that flow from the valley's uppermost reaches and are home to abundant freshwater aquatic life. From these shores at certain times of the year, the ancient Hawaiians that lived here would paddle their outrigger canoes to the Kalaupapa Peninsula and then proceed on foot to Moomomi to catch fish, where it was dried and later transported back to their villages.

▲ Moku Manu is a small, spiked pinnacle of lava rock jutting upward from the ocean's surface. Only a hundred yards offshore, it is barren of all vegetation and further dramatizes this beautiful virgin area. The occasional fisherman that does venture to this far end of the coast will usually have a good size fish on his line if he cruises by this rock with several lures in the water. ▶

◄

A small waterfall in Haupu Bay has been steadily cutting a wire-drawn line through this cliff for many years. As time passes, the water-fall itself will cease to exist, as the waters cut their thin path through the rock to reach the sea below.

Anapuhi Cave is large enough to pass a good size boat through its interior. Legend has it that the second opening in the rear was caused by a fierce battle between an enormous eel who lived there and guarded all of Molokai's North Shore, and a giant shark that wanted to claim the cave for himself. So great was their rolling and twisting fight that they tore clear through the solid rock to the other side of the cliff.

▼

▲ Kukaiwaa Point, nearing the Kalaupapa Peninsula and the end of Molokai's "backside." June through August is the best time to make this trip, because of wind and water conditions. The weather, however, is unpredictable and can change overnight, from a calm ocean and clear blue skies to 30-knot winds with 15-foot seas and sullen, foreboding horizons.

▲ From the coastal waters along the Kalaupapa Peninsula, with Okala Island just offshore, the view is just as spectacular looking east toward Halawa as it is at Halawa looking west. Near here in the district of Kalawao is where the first lepers were pushed from the decks of the ships that brought them to this isolated place and literally made to swim for their very lives to the Kalaupapa Peninsula.

CHAPTER 6 · KALAUPAPA PENINSULA

▼▼▼▼▼▼▼▼▼▼▼▼▼▼▼▼▼▼▼▼▼▼▼▼▼▼▼▼▼▼▼▼▼▼▼

Kalaupapa is a small peninsula of 4 1/2 square miles, jutting out from the high sea cliffs that dominate the windward coast of Molokai. The area was formed by a volcano called Kauhako about half a million years ago, thousands of years after the rolling hills to the southwest and the rugged mountain ranges to the southeast were forged by fiery eruptions. Its shores are craggy and weatherbeaten to the east, placid and accessible by boats to the west.

A small community of native Hawaiians populated a village on the western coastal area of Kalaupapa for hundreds of years before the days of leprosy. They raised sweet potatoes in the rocky soil throughout the peninsula, protecting their crops from the strong winds by building low rock walls, many of which are still visible today. Some of the crops and hogs they raised on the windswept plains were traded with Hawaiians from nearby valleys for different foods to supplement their diet. In fact, during the California Gold Rush, ships often stopped at Kalaupapa to barter with the Hawaiians for these crops for the crew's consumption.

In 1865 Kalaupapa was chosen by King Kamehameha V as an appropriately remote and inaccessible site for leprosy patients. An increasing number of Hawaiians had become infected with leprosy, as they had little resistance to disease not present before the advent of the white man in the early 1800's.

The leprosy patients were literally dropped off in the rough ocean on the eastern coast and settled there, living in hunger, loneliness and despair. As patients drifted westward from that inhospitable shore, the Hawaiian villagers gradually left. Some relocated to other areas of Molokai by choice, and others were evicted by the government.

Beginning in 1887 and ending in 1932, the settlement facilities - boys' and girls' homes, hospital, and administrative offices - were gradually removed from the windward eastern coast to their present area which offers more protection from the blistering winds.

Kalaupapa is perhaps best known for the work of "The Martyr of Molokai," Father Damien DeVeuster. He volunteered in 1873 to serve the leper settlement on a rotating basis, but once there, decided to remain. Damien brought law and order to the lives of the patients and the family members who accompanied them. He provided nursing help, spiritual care and consolation to the living and buried their wasted bodies after they died. Father Damien was a religious missionary, a skilled carpenter, and an able organizer who relieved many of the stresses upon the residents there.

He contracted leprosy in 1884 and remained in Kalaupapa to continue his service to those who needed him. The Martyr died of leprosy at the age of 49, after devoting the last sixteen years of his life to the patients at Kalaupapa. He will never be forgotten. The Roman Catholic Church is thoroughly examining Damien's personal life, his writings and his ministry. After these investigations, he will officially become the saint that many have already regarded him to be since he entered Kalaupapa.

Today, many visitors enter Kalaupapa by plane, but some visitors enter by means of a switchback trail from "Topside" Molokai. The top of the trail affords a glorious view of the whole peninsula, the forbidding cliffs and the seas that border it. The old buildings are still visible, many now abandoned to the brush that springs up seemingly overnight when tenants leave.

For the patients' use there is a store, a bar, a service station and a small post office, but very little else, other than their homes, the administration buildings and a hospital. Today, there is new energy from the National Park Service, restoring and preserving old sites, preparing for the day when the state Department of Health will no longer have jurisdiction over the settlement.

The right of patients to remain there for their lifetime is protected by Federal law. Although a few older patients remain in Kalaupapa today, they are free to come and go as their health allows. Since 1946, sulfur drug treatment has controlled Hansen's Disease and since 1969, the patients are no longer required to be confined to the settlement.

Now, Kalaupapa is free of the horrors and heartache once endured there, and its tranquil beauty dominates as before.

Kalaupapa Peninsula is an extremely flat and isolated portion of Molokai that is surrounded by a deep, violent ocean on three sides and virtually unscalable sheer cliffs on the fourth side. The powerful northeast tradewinds continually rake across this harsh and rocky land with relentless indifference to both man and beast.

The peninsula was formed about half a million years ago, long after the rolling hills of the West End and the rugged mountains to the east. It was created by the now extinct Kauhako Volcano, whose height gradually rises over the otherwise flat terrain to a height of 405 feet above sea level. Within the crater is a brackish lake that descends to 400 feet below sea level and provides a habitat for several types of native Hawaiian shrimp. Along the steep vertical walls ascending from the lake, a thick forest of trees cling stubbornly to an almost impossible life.

For supplies that the residents of Kalaupapa need on a daily basis, or more frequently than the twice a year supply barge, there is a tiny airstrip on the northwestern tip of the peninsula. Although the short runway is now paved, the author can remember in the early days of his flying career when there was no asphalt. You simply landed on the grass. What happens if you run out of runway? Well, this is what both ends of the airstrip look like, even today.

▲ Originally, the leprosy settlement was at Kalawao on the windward, southeastern side of the peninsula from 1865 until 1932. It was moved to its present location largely due to the fact that the new area provided more shelter from the raging winds and had calmer waters on which ships brought supplies for the settlement.

◀

Protecting passing ships from the jagged coastline during pitch black nights, the Kalaupapa Light House began service in 1909. Its 620,000 candlepower, three-ton Fresnel lens was manufactured in England and could be seen for 21 miles at sea. The lens, however, was replaced in 1985 by a newer type of automatic rotating beacon. The six window-like openings allow sunlight around the 189-step staircase.

▶ From the settlement's small wharf the view gives a much more imposing sight of the sheer descending walls on which the switchback trail is located. Most of the peninsula's coast, with the exception of Awahua Beach, is composed of unapproachable, jagged lava outcroppings, boulders and "white water" such as this.

Whether you hike or ride a mule down to the Kalaupapa Settlement, at trail's end you will be greeted to this spectacular view of Awahua Bay and the vertical cliffs, leading to the Moomomi Preserve to the west. The area of land above these towering cliffs is commonly called "Topside."

▼

The only gas station around, yet there is never a waiting line at the pump! On the supply barge twice a year, gasoline for automobiles and many other uses is brought ashore in 55-gallon drums in which it is stored until it is needed by the population.

Having been sent to Kalaupapa as a very young boy, this man now is one of the guides for visitors entering the settlement. Behind him is the only store on the peninsula which is state owned and operated by the patients themselves.

St. Francis is the present day Catholic Church serving Kalaupapa. Its site is where Our Lady Health of the Sick Church once stood, from 1881 to 1906. The beautiful wooden building was destroyed by a fire that entirely consumed the structure in 35 minutes. Construction of the new rock and cement church was completed in 1908.

Silhouetted against the high cliffs, Kanaana Hou United Church of Christ serves the needs of the Mormon community within the settlement.

A Celtic cross of red granite, dedicated to Father Damien and Brother Dutton, was donated in 1893 by the people of England. It is inscribed in both English and Hawaiian: " Greater love hath no man than this, that he lay down his life for his friends. John 15."

◄ The neatly kept grave site of Mother Marianne, a name known world-wide. She arrived at the settlement five months before the death of Father Damien in 1889. She was a nurse, educator and excellent administrator who devoted the next 29 years of her life to improving the education and welfare of the patients exiled there.

Two small lava rocks with a pearl of wisdom painted on their side lie on the grass near the site where Mother Marianne is buried.
▼

▶ This bronze statue of the Sacred Heart was an anonymous donation to St. Francis' Church. Buried at its base is the grave of Father Maxine Andre, who for twenty years lived and worked in Kalaupapa during the early 1900's. The statue is kept painted white because of the large amount of salt in the air.

Siloama Congregational Church, The Church of the Healing Springs, was built in Honolulu in 1872 and was shipped in sections to Kalawao where it was erected. In 1885 it was rebuilt, and its front was rotated 90 degrees to face west, away from the harsh winds. Due to being ravaged by both storms and termites, the wooden structure was again renovated in 1966.
▼

St. Philomena Church, also located in Kalawao, was built by Father Damien in 1876 and enlarged to its present size in 1888. The interior of the church looks very much the same today as it did when it was originally built, including the holes in the floor Father Damien cut by hand, so that the lepers with lung problems could spit during services.

Appearing peaceful and tranquil with its window to the North Shore, Kalawao was once a place of great pain and hardship, where those with leprosy were forced to swim to shore from the ships that transported them here, with only several days' food supply. Those that survived to reach the coast were greeted to a wasteland, void of shelters, food and doctors. It was a cruel and lawless time, where the strong preyed upon the weak and only the strongest survived.

A photograph of Father Damien as a young priest hangs on an aged wall of St. Joseph's Church which he built in 1876.

Father Damien died from complications of leprosy in 1889 and at his request was buried beside his beloved St. Philomena Church near where he spent his first night at Kalaupapa under a hala tree. His remains were exhumed in 1936 and returned to his homeland at the request of the Belgian government. Today, plans are underway for the Pope of the Roman Catholic Church to present a relic (a portion of Damien's remains) wrapped in a special kapa cloth, reserved only for alii, to a delegation from Hawaii. Sealed in a special metal box, it will be returned to Molokai and reinterred at Father Damien's original grave site in Kalawao.

▲ The top of Kauhako Crater, called Puu Uao Lookout, offers a panoramic 360° view of the entire Kalaupapa Peninsula. The white cross on the crest of the crater was constructed to hold Easter sunrise services and is visible for miles around in any direction.

▲ This area, rich in archaeological sites, was populated by Hawaiians for hundreds of years before the arrival of the lepers and has remained relatively untouched by "outside hands." There are miles after miles of low-lying rock walls that were used as windbreaks for crops, pens for raising pigs, and perhaps as property boundaries. On the southeastern slope of the crater, this heiau's purpose is unknown, but it did command both a powerful and magnificent vista, facing the imposing walls that isolate Kalaupapa.

Across the dome of Kauhako, there are a number of burial crypts, most of them without names or dates. It is estimated that there are almost 10,000 unmarked graves on this lonely windswept peninsula, names and lifetimes forever erased from memory by the passing of time. ▶

CHAPTER 7 · FLOWERS AND PLANTS

▼▼▼▼▼▼▼▼▼▼▼▼▼▼▼▼▼▼▼▼▼▼▼▼▼▼▼▼▼▼▼

For the most part, plants that are associated with being from Hawaii are in actuality plants that have been introduced to the islands over the last several centuries by outside contact. With the abundant rainfall, sunshine and unequaled climate, alien plants both good and bad have adapted readily to their life in the tropics, growing profusely in practically every district.

In a land that does not have the wide seasonal changes, the annual growth in certain areas, if left unchecked, can result in a dense jungled effect within a short period of time, completely engulfing not only the terrain, but structures as well.

Propagation of plant life is quite easily achieved in this ideal year-'round climate. Seeds left on the ground and cuttings merely pushed into the earth quickly spring into life. Practically anyone in Hawaii that has available soil can have a "green thumb" if they choose to, whether they grow flowers, fruit trees or a vegetable garden.

There are a little over a thousand species of native flora existing in Hawaii today, some rare and endangered, others quite beautiful and worthy of being seen. For the most part, however, they grow in isolated areas where man and his introduced animals and insects do not intrude, deep in the bogs of the rain forest, on steep cliffs where seemingly no life could exist, and sometimes in a controlled environment that man himself has created to ensure their survival for future generations.

The following examples represent a small sampling of the diverse plant life that grows throughout Molokai and is not representative of true Hawaiian flora, but rather a sampling of some of the more beautiful plants and flowers that have, over the decades, become associated with being "Hawaiian."

▲ Bougainvillea is a common shrub seen on Molokai. Its rapid growing, woody vine gives off massed clusters of small, paper-like flowers. During the flowering season, it becomes a solid barricade of living color, making it the focal point of a hillside or garden.

▲ Made of fuchsia and white bougainvillea with a sprinkling of green ferns, this Molokai woman has created her lei to match the pareau (sarong) she wears. This cool, loose-fitting garment is very popular with the women of Hawaii. It can be tied in a variety of ways, each creating its own individual look.

◀

Commonly called "Blue Ginger," this succulent evergreen imported from Brazil can grow to a height of about 8 feet. The plant, with its brilliant, purplish blue flower clusters, can be found in some of our less sunlit Molokai gardens.

Ever-blooming Kimi Pink Ginger thrives in Molokai's shaded gardens. Its rosy floral head grows at the end of the rich green foliage stalks. The long, leathery-leaf blades often grow to two feet in length. Its blooms are long-lasting when cut and are grown both commercially for export and for local floral arrangements.

▼

▲ White ginger, known to Hawaiians as Awapuhi Keokeo, is one of the most pleasing of all ginger. The large blossoms are commonly strung into leis or produced into perfume. Just a few cut flowers will permeate an entire area with their sweet scent. They can be found growing wild in Molokai's lush, wet forest regions, and can reach a height of about 7 feet.

▲ This shrub, or small tree, with its clusters of showy fuchsia-colored flowers is a tropical Rhododendron. The leaves are small and leathery, almost evergreen, on stalks of woody branches. Colors can vary, from a light pink and fuchsia to purple, yellow, salmon and white. They flourish and prosper abundantly throughout Molokai.

▲ There are many different shapes, colors and sizes of Bromeliad, an epiphyte that thrives on air as well as soil. They are found throughout Hawaii, and are sometimes called air plants.

▶ Looking almost artificial, the Anthurium, with its shiny, waxy flower, is one of the most widely recognized plants in Hawaii. Grown on Molokai in damp and shady areas, their colors range from purple, deep red, orange, pink, white and green. Sizes range from miniatures to this giant variety. When cut, they are long lasting, making them ideal for shipment to the mainland for a special occasion.

◄ Hawaii's state flower is the widely known hibiscus. There are vast numbers of hybrids in existence, all different in color and floral form. This beautifully colored orange-pink Sunburst is of the single petal variety, spanning 8 inches across.

◄ Most common of all hibiscus varieties is the red, also known as the Chinese Hibiscus which, if left unpruned, can reach a height of 20 feet. Hibiscus shrubs bloom year 'round and best after a heavy rain. The flowers of most varieties open early in the morning and later close as the sun sets. A few varieties will last as long as 3 days. In Polynesian culture, a flower worn over the right ear shows that a person is looking for a mate; if worn over the left ear, the mate has been found.

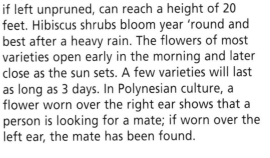

▲ A large double-petaled Snow White hibiscus variety is shown here. Hibiscus are easily grown and commonly seen in many Molokai's front yards. This flower, when cut, lasts but a single day.

More than 33 varieties of hibiscus from around the world have been crossed with the Hawaiian varieties to produce more than 5,000 cultivated varieties. This yellow-orange hybrid with its red center is an ornamental which can vary in color and form across the island chain. Some are double petaled and very large, ranging in colors from pale yellow to deep orange-yellow, true orange and orange red, along with many combinations of these and other colors.

This pink fruited banana is a dwarf species in comparison to most banana plants. Its velvety pink fruits are interesting in that as they ripen, they gradually peel themselves back, exposing their creamy flesh. These bananas are inedible and are grown as ornamentals to be used in large exotic floral arrangements.

▲ The Ixora, or "Jungle Flame," blooms most of the year, producing a round snowball head of tiny, four-petal flowers. The blooms of these small bushes range from white to a deep crimson red, and have a pleasant but mild smell.

▲ Suggesting a "bird in flight" with its beautiful crested plumage, this popular flower, the Bird of Paradise, makes an attractive cut flower lasting as long as two weeks. If left on the plant, about 6 blossoms will emerge, one every other day, making the plant grow more spectacular and brighter with color each day.

◄

The impressive Chenille plant is actually a small ornamental tree that can reach a height of about 12 feet. It yields deep red fur-like flower clusters which resemble monkey tails. The tails, which grow as long as 18 inches, are made up of staminate flowers which have no petals. This most unusual and beautiful shrub, with its dark green pointed leaves, bears its velvety clusters throughout most of the year.

Queen Flower, otherwise known in Hawaii as the Kalihi Flower, is a species of the Crepe Myrtle. Its scentless lavender-pink flowers bloom in masses during the summer months and can grow to 10 feet or more, depending on soil conditions. Flowers on this shrub appear in large, loose, upright heads at the branch tips, which display a frilled, ruffled and crepe like appearance.

Night Blooming Cereus is actually a Mexican cactus plant. It has thick, scalloped, 3-sided spiny stems, which can be seen climbing up walls, banks, and even making its way into trees, sometimes to a height of 60 feet. Buds usually begin to form in June. Between June and October, the large buds open after dark and remain open until the morning heat wilts them and they droop to a close.

▲ The Royal Poinciana, also known as Ohai Alii in Hawaii, is a flowering tree bursting with a mass of vivid red blossoms throughout the spring and summer months. It comes in other color combinations as well and if grown in favorable conditions, this graceful tree, with its leathery fern-like leaves, can reach a height of 40 feet. Heavy, long seed pods can be seen draping on the tree three months after blooming, pulling the branches down by their weight, giving this tree an umbrella-like appearance.

◀

Frequently covering the ground with color are the fluted and irregular lobes of the Pink Tecoma tree. It is said to have been introduced to Hawaii from different parts of South America. The blooming season is unpredictable; some years, the tree is covered in a mass of pink flowers, and at other times only a few buds will actually bloom.

The Crown of Thorns, one of many euphorbias, is another attractive ornamental which grows from about 1 to 4 feet in height. A native of Madagascar, it produces very long, sharp thorns on round, succulent stems. It bears jewel-like flower clusters year 'round. According to legend, the flower bracts, commonly red in color, are said to have changed from their original white to red after the plant was worn as the Crown by Jesus Christ.

▼

▲ Growing wild in many parts of Molokai are these often seen Ilima plants. They resemble a small hibiscus flower and range from a pale yellow to orange and brown. Their small, papery blossoms are frequently strung into leis by threading them through the center. They were formerly known as the "Royal" lei, since only chiefs were allowed to wear them.

▲ Growing to heights of 9 feet, the Golden Parrot heliconia blooms year 'round. The bloom itself is about 7 inches long. This makes an excellent cut flower, because of its lasting beauty.

An exceptional exotic tropical plant, the "Red Giant" heliconia, grows to about 20 feet in height. Its banana-like leaves and sturdy leaf stalks make for a dramatic addition to any flower exhibit. The waxy flowers grow from about 9 inches across to 15 or more inches in length.

◄

Another pendant heliconia, Heliconia Chartacea, more commonly called "Sexy Pink," is a beautiful example of a tropical exotic. With its long bloom cascading downward, it can have as many as 28 bracts. This one is about 20 inches in length. Its stalks and foliage grow to about 16 feet and with its exotic appeal, it makes the focal point of any large tropical floral arrangement.

This beautiful species, Heliconia Rostrata, grows pendant-like from its stalk. The plant can reach a height of 20 feet. Originating from Amazonian Peru and Ecuador, its crimson red bracts, at times totaling up to 35, have a fluorescent yellow-green lip. Here, they have reached a length of about 16 inches, making it an exquisite addition to any floral display.

▼